Patti's Journey In Faith

By
Evelyn Wagner

TEACH Services, Inc.
PUBLISHING
www.TEACHServices.com

Copyright © 2009, Revised 2012 TEACH Services, Inc.
ISBN-13: 978-1-57258-598-0 (Paperback)
ISBN-13: 978-1-57258-839-4 (ePub)
ISBN-13: 978-1-57258-840-0 (Kindle/Mobi)

Library of Congress Control Number: 2009927582

Published by
TEACH Services, Inc.
P U B L I S H I N G
www.TEACHServices.com

DEDICATION

To my parents,
Otto and Marjorie Mitchell,
whose love and prayers
have always ascended to God for us.

Thank you, Rita McMullen,
for the inspiration and encouragement
that brought this book to life.

I also want to thank the many
friends and relatives who read
the manuscript and gave
advice and encouragement.

FOREWORD

Patti's Journey in Faith is the true story of a couple named Delmer and Evelyn, but known as Del and Patti in this setting, and their struggle to serve their Lord in the challenges of a new marriage, going to college, and then starting a new business.

We meet them at Walla Walla College (University now) and go with them through a life of love, courage, disappointment, laughter, and discovery with the overarching theme of the gracious nearness of God.

—Ruthanneke Edwards

Table of Contents

1

Beginnings

Patti sat in her small living room quietly marveling how the Lord had been leading Del and her since their marriage on June 14, 1953, just a few short months ago. She watched the gathering darkness as it slowly covered the outside world and could hear the animated voices of her neighbors through the thin wall of her apartment. This place definitely would not be featured in *Better Homes and Gardens*, but Patti felt fortunate to be able to move into this older apartment building filled with young married students going to Walla Walla College.

Last spring after their wedding, she and Del had sold books in Canada during their summer vacation. The scholarships they earned helped pay for their college tuition and for their apartment furnished only with a small stove and refrigerator.

The day before yesterday, Patti's Uncle Frank had backed his truck up to the door. She ran to greet him and heard him say, "You know, I happen to have some extra furniture here. It has been used some, but I thought you wouldn't mind keeping it for me."

Patti had not questioned why he had extra furniture. The one small table and two chairs fit perfectly into the miniature kitchen. There was a couch with matching chair and also a rocking chair that Uncle Frank brought in for the living room. When the bed and large dresser were unloaded and arranged, Patti felt the empty apartment had truly been transformed into a home.

Her heart had been singing as she waved good-bye to Uncle Frank and watched him drive down the road. The apartment had been so bare, and they had no money to buy furniture, but look at it now! Cozy and comfortable!

Patti stood, admiring the dark-blue velvet couch. It never entered her mind that Uncle Frank and Aunt Agnes had bought that furniture for them to use; hand picked it to fit into the apartment perfectly.

She had been saving all the loose change that she found during the summer. Sometimes when she had washed Del's clothes, she had found that his pockets were filled with change from the down payments he received from selling books. This money had been stashed away in a little green cut-glass jar that was kept in the back of the cupboard. Yesterday she had surprised Del and told him about the money. They had counted it together. Thirty dollars! With the money and the many jars of fruit her mother had canned for them, they would have plenty to eat until Del's first paycheck arrived.

"But my God shall supply all your need according to His riches in glory by Christ Jesus." Philippians 4:19. What a promise!

That afternoon Del had come home, changed his clothes, grabbed his lunch and dashed to the car. Patti watched him go down the road on his way to pick up five other fellows who also worked an eight hour shift at Harris Pine Mills in Pendleton, Oregon—forty miles away.

Why did I tell Del, when making his lunch the other morning, that I usually just go to the corner store and buy a pint of ice cream in the evening? It doesn't cost much and tastes so-o-o good. He seemed very upset. "You eat only ice cream for a whole meal every night?"

"Why not? It is only 25 cents—the cheapest thing I can buy. It makes a delicious meal."

"Don't you ever think about your health?" He appeared absolutely frustrated at the thought.

No, Patti had not been thinking much about that part of it. She had grown up on the farm where they raised a big garden. They lived out of it all summer while preserving fruits and vegetables for the next winter. On the farm a person didn't need to spend much money for groceries. They seldom had desserts. Ice cream was a treat for holidays. Now Del expected her to spend good money for plain old vegetables when she could be having a treat every evening!

2

College Daze

Patti quietly slipped out of bed in the early morning darkness. It was a little before six, and since Del had not gotten home from work until after two-thirty that morning, she must let him sleep as long as he could.

Pop! Rattle! Crackle! Bang!

Oh, no. Why do these old pipes have to sound like they are bursting with excess energy when the hot water surges through them?

A warm shower finished off with cold water made Patti feel wide awake. She got ready for class and started breakfast before calling Del. A few moments later the sound of Del's tenor voice mixed with running water drifted from the shower.

She set dishes on the table and opened a jar of fruit. *He radiates vigor and exuberance like sunbeams,* she mused. *I don't know how he can be so cheerful after getting so little sleep.*

After the oatmeal cooked and breakfast was finished, Del hastily gathered his books, gave her a quick kiss, and hurried out the door to his seven-thirty class. With the kitchen clean, Patti collected her books and walked the few blocks to the college campus.

Her fingers flew in Typing II. But Shorthand II—*oh, dear.*

Why couldn't she ever get it all down so she could read it back? After struggling through shorthand class, she hurried out of the administration building to start an exciting and challenging part of the day—working at the library. Patti had desperately wanted to get a job in the college library, so one of the first classes she signed up for at the college was Library Science taught by Miss Blackney. Years before, she had promised herself that someday, someway, she would work in that very place surrounded by books, magazines, and knowledge. She would learn everything she could on how to locate the information available and then share it with anyone who asked for her help. She would let no one leave the library feeling crushed and bewildered the way she had felt when, in the tenth grade, she entered the college library for the first time. The girl working at the desk that day was not only unfriendly and abrupt, but she was absolutely rude.

Now Patti had this coveted job, and she loved working with the other students and anyone else needing her help. She made new friends at work and wanted to get better acquainted with Donna, a vivacious and agreeable new girl, who had just started working at the library. Patti knew they would have a lot of fun together.

It was after nine-forty on this particular evening by the time the library closed and everything had been put in order. Donna and her friend, Barbara, chatted with Patti on the steps of the building before heading for the dormitory.

"Where do you live?" Donna looked at Patti.

"Down in the Veterans' Apartments."

"You're going to walk all that way down there by yourself this time of night?" Donna appeared alarmed.

Patti nodded.

"You can't walk all that way by yourself. I'll come with you."

"Then I'll come too." Barbara turned toward Donna. "You would have to come back by yourself. That would be as bad as Patti going by herself in the first place."

Donna and Barbara were fun friends, and now they were including her. *Thank you, Lord.* High-spirited and happy the girls talked and laughed all the way to Patti's home. She unlocked the door, and her dark little apartment came to life with a flip of a light switch. Patti heard her friends gasp. Looking surprised, both girls walked straight over to a picture of her and Del smiling out at them.

"Are you married?" Barbara picked up the picture.

"Didn't you know that?" Patti laughed.

"Is that your husband? Is that really your husband?" Donna looked like she had just gone into shock.

"Of course it's her husband." Barbara had a look of triumph. "It's her wedding picture, isn't it?"

"Oh." Donna spoke quietly to Barbara, as Patti left the room to prepare them something hot to drink. The girls continued talking in low tones. Patti felt they were talking about her, or Del—or—*what in the world were they talking about?*

Barbara walked over to Patti laughing. Patti saw a look of victory on Barbara's face. But Donna—she looked like pure misery, a fervent desire to be somewhere else at this moment.

Barbara's laugh filled the living room and danced around the walls. "Donna has been telling me about this really cute guy who comes into the library to study during the ten-thirty morning period." Barbara grinned at Donna. Her glee bubbled out filling the room with laughter. Then Barbara stopped and drew a long breath.

Patti's body began to tighten, and she felt dreadfully uncomfortable.

3

Goals

Patti glanced at Donna. She was not laughing, and Patti could see she felt extremely unhappy.

"Well—." Barbara giggled. "This guy is always by himself, and Donna said he seemed really neat." Barbara stopped again, enjoying the suspense of the moment. The stillness of the night lay all around, but Barbara's merriment, deaf to entreaties, glowed with delight as she continued, "Donna made a bet with me that this cute guy—well, your husband— would be asking her for a date before the girl's banquet."

The teakettle whistled unheeded. Embarrassment consumed Donna's every move. Patti was speechless. She could have congratulated Donna for knowing a neat, cute guy when she saw one. She could have made Donna feel better, but she didn't. Frustration captured her body, fogging her brain and clouding her thoughts. She thanked the girls for accompanying her home and walked with them to the door. Then she locked it for the night behind them. What Barbara said left Patti puzzled and disturbed. Now she and Donna would probably never be friends.

Do I want to be friends? Slowly she headed for bed with weighted feet.

At work Patti tried to be friendly with Donna, but she acted cool and indifferent. One day Patti noticed that Donna wasn't around. She had not seen her for days or weeks. Had she changed jobs? Had she quit school? Patti never knew, and it haunted her like the memory of some former happiness.

Del's eight-week, temporary job at Harris Pine Mills had been a Godsend. He had been getting very little sleep, but that first paycheck seemed to compensate for the hours of hard work.

"Oh, Del." Patti threw her arms around her husband. "Just think, now we can make the car payment and also the payment on the little camper we lived in last summer. I have been so concerned."

"Yes." Del held her close. "We certainly can use this check. But it isn't going to go very far with all the bills we have to pay."

"I only need to get one thing." She stood back and looked at him. "I need a dustpan. That is all I plan to buy."

"We don't have that much money."

"What?!"

"We won't have money left to buy anything." Del looked sad.

"That isn't right. I have to have a dustpan. I sweep every room in the house and have been sweeping the dirt onto a piece of paper too long. A dustpan doesn't cost very much. This is ridiculous! We could at least buy that!"

Del stood quietly looking at Patti. He did not say a word, but studied her with a strange expression covering his face.

Oh, my, what have I done? He works so hard at Harris Pine Mills and is always so cheerful. Patti's heart ached for she loved Del dearly, and now she had hurt him deeply. She could tell by the look in his eyes.

Del reached into his pocket, pulled out his wallet, found his paycheck, signed it, and handed it to her.

"Stretch it as far as you can."

Patti gasped. "Thank you, Honey. I'll do my best." She knew how to stretch money. First the tithe, next she paid the bills and then—well then—the money was all gone. Miraculously that paycheck had covered all the pressing bills!! *Thank You, God. Oh, well—she would be able to get a dustpan later. It wasn't that hard to sweep the dirt from the floor onto the piece of paper before dumping it into the garbage.*

When Del's temporary job came to an end, Patti knew she had better try to get a job at the Corps of Engineers. Three of her friends had passed the government test and gone to work to put their husbands through college. But Patti could not pass the shorthand section. Her shorthand teacher, Miss Walker, gave her extra help, but it was no use. Patti failed the test every time she took it.

Miss Walker called Patti into her office. "Would you and Del be willing to move into F.W. Peterson's house? He travels most of the time since his wife died. He needs a young couple whom he can trust to live at his place. It would be a great opportunity for you to meet a lot of important people. The basement is full of canned food. The cupboards are full of groceries. You could use everything as if it belonged to you. When F.W. Peterson is home, you need just put on an extra dish. He is not a big eater, and he likes things simple."

Frank W. Peterson had been the Business Manager of Walla Walla College for thirty-four years. Because of his rare business ability and outstanding management, the college had developed and achieved remarkable advancement during those years.

Patti left Miss Walker's office with her thoughts busy as a hive of bees. Could this be God's answer to their prayers? They always needed more groceries, and now they were being offered a house full of food.

Del and Patti drove to Mrs. Neff's to get her opinion. Mrs. Neff, grandmother to Cousin Jean, was their friend and mentor. Patti, her brother Bob, and Jean had lived at Mrs. Neff's for three years while attending Walla Walla Valley Academy. Del had learned to confide in Mrs. Neff a few years previously. When Patti had gotten angry with him and refused to date him during their early college days, he had come to see Mrs. Neff.

"Start dating the nicest girl in school," she had told him. "Date someone Patti really admires. Don't be so discouraged. You will get her back."

Sometime later, Patti was in the big restroom at school and heard this pretty, talented girl talking to her friend and telling her about this wonderful guy she had dated the past weekend. The two girls stood combing their hair in front of the large mirrors. Patti could see them through the crack by the door but stayed where she was until they both had left the room.

She felt concern for this girl, because she knew her hopes would soon be dashed to the ground. Patti didn't think it was very thoughtful of Del to do this to such a nice girl and had no idea it was all Mrs. Neff's fault. Now while they drove to her home they knew whatever she told them would be sound advice.

While Mrs. Neff's late husband had been president of the North Pacific Union Conference many people at the college had become acquainted with her and learned the value of her counsel.

Mrs. Neff listened carefully as Patti told of the offer they had received to move into the beautiful home of F.W. Peterson. She rocked slowly and quietly as though hearing about this adventure for the first time. Then she said, "When Myrtle Walker asked about you two, I told her that it was one of the smartest things she had ever thought of."

Patti was aghast. "Really? That is a lot of responsibility. I'm terribly afraid."

"You can do it." Mrs. Neff smiled. "Never forget, if you need any help, I will help you in any way I can.

4

Moving

"This is your bedroom." F.W. Peterson showed Del and Patti a beautiful room and gave them a few words of encouragement before he left on an extended vacation. Mrs. Hazel Peterson, F.W.'s sister-in-law, and Miss Walker came over to make sure that everything was in order and to help Patti get settled.

"Just mix your groceries right in with what is here," Patti was instructed. "Please use all the food. When you move out, another young couple will take your place. Why leave it all to them?"

Patti poured her small sack of flour into the flour bin and picked up a sack of salt, thinking it contained sugar. It went into the sugar bin with no one realizing what she had done or imagining the consequences.

The next morning before eating the delicious breakfast spread out before them, Del's prayer was heartfelt and thankful. The freezer was nearly half filled with quarts of sweet, home-frozen strawberries. The refrigerator was full of food that wouldn't keep for long. And … why leave all of the other food that filled the cupboards for the next couple?

Patti created meals in a dream kitchen surrounded by culinary equipment she had never known existed. She baked big, crusty loaves of bread. They looked beautiful, but tasted—strange. Her bread had never had a flavor like this be-fore. She stuck the loaves into plastic bags and hid them in the back of the freezer. Why let F.W. be disappointed with her so soon?

The day F.W. came back, Patti spent extra time in the kit-chen preparing an appealing meal. He had insisted that she must not go to any trouble for him. Ruskets and milk would be fine, but she knew that even her easy to please husband would not be satisfied with that. F.W. told them of the adven-tures of his travels, and again let Del and Patti know how special it was for him to have them there living in his home.

Patti left to get the dessert.

"Dessert!" F.W. exclaimed. "After a meal like that?"

She got the dessert plates from the cupboard and cut the freshly-made apple pie. It had been a lot of work, but that box of apples in the basement needed to be used, and she wanted this meal to be special. A small piece of pie fell to the side of the plate, so she picked it up and put it in her mouth.

Oh, no. It is terrible! She sampled another piece. *What is wrong?!* She felt like weeping. As she carefully sampled the third small piece of pie, she noticed that the pie had sort of a salty taste. Patti walked to the sugar bin and tasted its con-tents. *Yes, that is it! The sugar is mixed with salt! What should I do?* Now she knew why the bread tasted "different."

"Don't bring me a very big piece of dessert," F.W. called to her, "just a little one."

"Okay." She cut little slivers of pie and smothered them with some ice cream she found in the freezer. Months later she told F.W. what happened. He laughed. "I knew some-thing had to be wrong with that pie, but I couldn't figure out what it might be."

Clyde Harris, founder of Harris Pine Mills, and F.W. went on a fishing trip. While they were gone, Mary Harris called to tell Patti that F.W. was so proud of her and Del.

"Last week he took us through the whole house showing us what a good housekeeper you are," she said. "He also took some bread out of the bread box and showed us the texture. He wanted to take some on the trip, but wouldn't do it without asking you first."

Clyde and Mary Harris had gone through the whole house to see how she kept it!!! How had it looked? And the bread … Oh, oh…

One evening F.W. Peterson sat down by Del. He hesitated a moment and then said, "I have a whole drawer of socks and will never be able to use all of them. I am not sure what to do with all those socks. Could you use any?"

Since Del did not answer, he continued. "Maybe I should give them to Dorcas so they could give them to someone who needs them."

"Maybe so." Del continued to concentrate on whatever he was working on.

Patti was horror-struck. *How could Del pass up such an opportunity?* As soon as F.W. was alone, she went to talk with him. "If you have any extra socks that you can't use, I will be glad to take them." She spoke quietly. He gave her a knowing smile and went to get a half dozen or so new socks from the dresser drawer in his bedroom.

"Thank you." She laid the socks in Del's dresser drawer beside his few other clean clothes. *"Now unto Him that is able to do exceeding abundantly above all that we ask or think…"* (Ephesians 3:20) came to Patti's mind. *Of course F.W. couldn't help but have noticed that I wash out Del's one pair of socks every night so he will have a clean pair to put on the next morning. Now his socks can be washed with the rest of the clothes in the washing machine.*

Del searched in vain for another night job after his temporary job at Harris Pine Mills came to an end. Patti did not register for classes spring quarter. She knew she had to find a cash-paying job

5

New Experiences

WANTED: PART-TIME SECRETARY.
Some telephone work required. Must
have good typing and shorthand skills.

OOPS! Why did every job want someone who was good in shorthand? I'll apply for the job anyway. Who knows how good "good" needs to be?

She rode the bus to Walla Walla to meet a two o'clock appointment that Friday afternoon and stepped into the elevator that took her to the third floor of the Book Nook Building. Mrs. G., a large bustling woman, greeted Patti as she hesitantly stepped into the capacious, well-kept office that overlooked the street below. The hurried, unorganized interview was over before she thought it had begun. "I must be leaving right away." Mrs. G. arose, and Patti also stood. "I have three applications here that look good. When I get back, I will decide whom I wish to hire and will let you know." Mrs. G. quickly gathered her things and stuffed them into a bag. Patti walked from the room wondering what chance she had of getting a job in this spacious office.

The next Monday morning Patti answered the telephone and heard an unfamiliar voice. "Hello. Is this Patti? I'm Hazel calling from the G & D Insurance Company. Mrs. G. told me she plans to hire you for the secretarial job that I have."

22

"She does?" Patti tried to keep her excitement to a normal level. "I didn't know anyone filled that position yet. What do you mean 'the job you have'? Mrs. G. talked as if she needed to get someone immediately to take care of the office."

"That is right." Hazel's voice sounded a little irritated. "She has hired several people already, but no one has been able to do the work. If you want to come down to the office today, I can start teaching you what needs to be done. That way you will have a whole week to learn before she gets back and starts confusing you."

Patti dressed in her best skirt and blouse and then caught the next bus into Walla Walla. *What am I getting into? Who is this person who invited me to the office? Why would she want to teach me the office procedure before I am officially hired?* She walked into the room with a head full of questions. An efficient looking woman a little older than Patti sat at the desk.

"This is really nice of you to take the time to teach me." Patti looked around the room half expecting Mrs. G. to be there somewhere.

"I am glad to help you." Hazel smiled. "But I am also doing this for myself. I told Mrs. G. that I would teach you this week. She said 'no.' She wanted to teach you herself to see how fast you can catch on. Let me tell you, if she teaches you, you will never catch on. She has just gone through four different secretaries, and either they quit or she fires them. Mrs. G. always begs me to come back to fill in. I am tired of it."

Patti listened as Hazel thoroughly explained each detail before going on to another. "Mrs. G. thinks this should be done another way, but don't forget what I am telling you. She can confuse you, and then be gone out on the road, and you won't know what to do. You'll get it. It just takes time. Don't ever, ever, tell her I taught you. Be sure to act as if she is the one teaching you."

6

The Working World

"Hello, Patti? This is Mrs. G. Could you be in the office by nine this morning? I would like to have you be in charge here. I want to get started right away teaching you what I want you to do."

Wow! Mrs. G. doesn't give much notice. Patti was ready, for she had been expecting that telephone call. Mentally she thanked Hazel for being such a scout.

As soon as Patti arrived at the office, Mrs. G. brought out all the books and laid them across the desk. She talked about one job and then another and then back to the first job in her authoritative, overpowering manner, but Hazel had prepared Patti. Mrs. G. seemed pleased with her progress, and Patti knew that she would always have a soft spot in her heart for Hazel.

On the fourth Monday morning of the job, (Mrs. G. thought it was the third) Mrs. G. said, "Patti, I think you understand what needs to be done and how to take care of the office. Today I will be leaving for a couple of weeks. I want you to start calling names in the phone book to make appointments for the salesman. You must cover a half-page a day. Mark each number you call so you will know where to start the next day. I want you to make at least one or two appointments every day. If you can do that, it will be good. You have heard me calling on the phone, so you should know how to do it.

"Oh, yes, there is one more thing I want you to do while I am gone. You must pay the bills that become due. Here is the checkbook. Just write the checks and sign my name."

"I can't sign your name!!" Patti was shocked.

"Sure you can. Here I will show you how. It will be easy." Mrs. G. wrote her name on a white piece of paper and held it up to the window with the check covering it. "See? Just copy my name and no one will know the difference."

"I cannot forge a check." Patti shuddered.

"It isn't forging if I ask you to do it."

When Mrs. G. had finished packing her things, she came over to the desk, pulled out the checkbook and signed a few checks. "I don't like doing this, but be sure to keep them where no one can take them." Then she was gone.

Patti sat at her desk dreading to start calling people she did not know, dreading to have them answer the phone, dreading to have them find out it was someone they did not know, and dreading to hear their reaction.

The reaction? Almost everyone acted friendly! Patti made appointments quickly. Still, she felt guilty disturbing somebody's happy day with her telephone call.

She thought her job was to get appointments—not to see how many names she could cross off in the telephone book. She stopped calling after making three appointments—for the salesman had told Patti not to get more than three a day.

The evening Mrs. G. returned from her two-week trip, the telephone rang. Patti could tell she was talking to an aggravated woman as soon as she heard Mrs. G.'s angry, "Hello, Patti?"

"Yes." Patti knew she was in big trouble. Now it seemed that even the pictures on the wall were frowning at her.

"I have been checking the phone book just to see if you have been doing your job." Mrs. G. was almost shouting. "I told you to cover half a page of names a day. You haven't even covered two pages all the time I have been gone. You have not been doing your job!"

The telephone receiver in Patti's hand seemed to be burning her ears.

"Well—what do you have to say for yourself?"

7

Conquering Fear

Patti thought a moment before answering. Obviously, Mrs. G. was not very happy with her.

"But, Mrs. G., you didn't expect me to get more than one or two appointments a day, and I've done that."

"That's not the point. I've done enough calling to know how much of the phone book you can cover in a day. I expect that much to be covered."

She gave her message, and before Patti could say another word—bang! The sound of Mrs. G. slamming down the telephone went straight through Patti's body. She stood by the telephone trying to comprehend the meaning of what had just happened.

Patti crumpled onto the couch. She was all alone and felt as dark as the world outside. All her efforts had been a failure. Her reward was blame and condemnation.

While Patti contemplated what had just happened, a decision, bathed in fire, slowly burnt itself into her mind. *Work, or no work, I will not make another telephone call getting people interested in the G & D Insurance Company—never, never, never!* She got up from the couch, walked over to the telephone, and picked up the receiver. Patti believed she had made a calm, quiet decision, but her hand trembled as she dialed Mrs. G.'s telephone number.

"I have decided that I cannot cover that much of the phone book. You may get someone else who can. I will not be in tomorrow morning." She dispatched her words in the smallest amount of time possible with the calmness of absolute fury.

Patti's watch said it was almost ten o'clock, and she needed some sleep. She slid between the cool pink sheets and closed her eyes, but the tears kept creeping out beneath her lashes. Del had so much energy and drive. Patti could never keep pace with the few hours of sleep he thrived on. Now she had even made a failure of her job. The tears soaked into the pillow under her head.

Suddenly the telephone shattered the stillness of the night. Patti threw a bathrobe on and went to answer it.

"You won't need to cover as much of the phone book as I do." Mrs. G. was talking rapidly. "I realize I'm pretty fast. We'll work something out."

"Thank you." Patti felt tired. "But I've put everything I had into trying to get appointments. It is something I really hate doing. I'm sure there are many people who would enjoy calling a lot more than I do."

The telephone rang long and insistently several times during the next hour, but Patti felt she knew who was on the other end of the line, and Mrs. G. was not her boss anymore.

Who would be calling at this early morning hour? It isn't even six o'clock yet. Patti slipped out of bed and went to answer the telephone.

"Hello, Patti," she heard a pleasant, but familiar voice say, "I have been thinking about what a good job you do taking care of the office. If you didn't have to do any solicitation calling on the phone, would you be willing to come back?"

"Well—ah—ah—well—ah—yes." Patti could hardly believe what she was hearing.

"Then will you come back today? You will not be required to do any phoning."

Oh, thank You, God, thank You. I still have a job!

Patti now had a job she really liked. Mrs. G. was gone most of the time. When she did come to the office, she actually acted as though she honestly appreciated whatever Patti did.

F.W. Peterson treated them as if he were living in their home. No wonder everyone liked him. Friends came and went, but they were never asked to stay for meals unless he checked to see if it was okay with Patti first.

"I am wondering—do you have a little extra food so we could invite Dr. and Mrs. D. to our place for lunch?" F.W. had a hopeful expression on his face.

8

Learning

Church was over, and Del and Patti were getting into F.W. Peterson's car to head home. Dr. and Mrs. D. had come to visit the College Place Church and F.W. was wishing to invite them over for lunch. Patti froze. What would she feed such a distinguished couple whom she didn't even know? She had already learned that F.W. really did prefer simple meals. Del seemed happy with them, so why should she spend so much time cooking? F.W. read Patti's face and headed the car for home.

"I haven't seen Dr. D. and his wife for years," F.W. reminisced. "He used to be president of the college."

Patti closed her eyes. *Dear, Lord, please help me know what to do.*

"Be not forgetful to entertain strangers: for thereby some have entertained angels unawares." Hebrews 13: 2.

"I think I figured out something for lunch," she brightened.

"Thank you." F.W. drove the car back to the church. Looking as hopeful as the break of day, he went into the building with hurried steps in anticipation that his friends were still there.

"They are already gone." He slowly climbed back into the car.

Oh, dear. Why hadn't she encouraged him to invite his friends home and then trusted in God to take care of the results? When would she ever learn?

Patti quickly prepared lunch. While F.W. and Del talked of things that were interesting to them, Patti's mind flew back to visions of another day. She could see herself when she had first gone to live at Mrs. Neff's.

"I am going to show you girls the proper way to entertain." Mrs. Neff spoke to Jean and Patti. "This weekend we are going to have Dr. Bowers, Dr. Sorenson, and Dr. Hendershot with their wives over for dinner. I want you two girls to set the table, help prepare the meal, and do the serving."

Patti listened with tense attention to Mrs. Neff's instructions to serve from the right and take the dishes away from the left, *or was it to serve from the left and take the dishes away from the right? Oh dear—and what else were they supposed to do?* This was a striking contrast to her idea of a fun afternoon.

"Do you think you are better than the guests that are coming tomorrow?" Jean asked Patti as they were walking into the dining room to set the table.

Patti clutched the stack of china plates she was carrying to keep them from falling to the floor. She looked at her cousin in utter amazement. *Why would she think of asking a thing like that? And that tone of her voice—it sounded very close to being sarcastic.*

"W-w-well—no," Patti stammered.

"Do you think they are better than you?"

"Well—I—guess—I—don't suppose so," muttered Patti.

"What makes one person better than another? Do you think it is money, prestige, or leadership? Well, I'll tell you what it is. It is character. The only way anyone can be better than you, is if that other person has a better character. If you don't have a good character, you'd better start doing something to improve it." Jean whirled around and went back into the kitchen while Patti finished setting the table.

Wow! Patti smiled to herself. *Mrs. Neff must have been talking to Jean so she wouldn't be afraid. I know Jean didn't figure all that out by herself.*

At that moment Patti's thoughts left all reminiscing behind and raced back to the present, for she heard F.W. say, "How would you two like to spend next weekend at the cabin at Wallowa Lake?"

9

Changes

A sleek-looking motor boat sat on a trailer that was hooked to the car, waiting to leave. "This is so exciting!" Patti gave Del a hug when he got home from work. "We are having a whole weekend at the lake and I don't have to cook a thing." They were going to the Peterson's cabin up in the woods by Wallowa Lake. Myrtle Walker had called Patti to let her know not to prepare any food for the weekend. She and Hazel Peterson would go up to the cabin early and have everything ready when F.W., Del, and Patti got there.

The cabin, snuggled under the large pine trees, overlooked the lake. Del and Patti walked the trails in the mountains that surrounded it. Del picked flowers and stuck them in Patti's hair. They sat at the water's edge and let it lap at their toes while they talked about things that were not very important and yet mattered tremendously. This was a reminder of their dating days, only now—now they had a lifelong date. They sat in front of the dancing fire in the fireplace and ate popcorn and listened to stories exchanged by the older people. Patti felt so much at home in this beautiful, simple setting. Her body soaked in the relaxing moments.

Sitting in the motor boat the next day, F.W. seemed to feel like a kid again as they cruised across the deep-blue lake to his friend's cabin. Arriving at the deck at Clyde and Mary

Harris's cottage, Patti saw Clyde out chopping wood. Mary was carrying a bucket of water after filling it from the hand pump on the back porch.

These wealthy people have to take a vacation to have the privilege of chopping wood and carrying water!!

That afternoon Clyde and F.W. had fun trying to outdo each other telling of days gone by. A relaxation and closeness that Patti had not felt before permeated the place. She watched Del play as hard as he worked, and life was fun.

The time flew, and all too soon F.W. and Del were hooking up the boat trailer to the car and loading the boat onto it. Then they were heading home again.

"I'll tell you a secret if you promise not to tell." F.W. spoke quietly.

"We can keep a secret." Anticipation filled the car.

"Myrtle Walker and I are very fond of each other," he confided in them.

"That is wonderful!" Patti smiled at F.W.

I've known that for a long time. Oh, dear. Now I've promised not to tell.

People had already started asking Del and Patti about their landlord's relationship with Miss Walker, and now their lips were sealed until the engagement was announced.

A few months later, on the day of the wedding, Del and Patti walked across the manicured lawn at Pastor and Mrs. Weaver's home. The organ was playing softly as people filled the rows of white folding chairs. Rose bushes peeked through the white picket fence while nearby white lilies nodded in the breeze.

The weather was lovely for an outdoor wedding. Patti looked around to see where Miss Walker would be coming from, and caught her breath. To the west, angry brown streaks of dust were sweeping towards the sky.

A gust of wind swept the sheet music across the audience. People were scrambling to catch the pieces before they got away. Two ushers rushed to the organ and held the music as the organist continued to play. Miss Walker made her way down the aisle. The wind increased with fury. People grabbed what they could and ran for the house following the bride and groom.

Four strong men grasped the organ and carried it quickly into the house, while others captured whatever was trying to fly away. People packed into every nook and cranny they could find inside and squeezed together to let others in out of the storm. With all the guests safely inside, the wedding continued. At the close of the ceremony, F.W. and the new Mrs. Peterson were showered with good wishes. They were two great people, who had spent their separate pasts helping others. Now they had joined their lives together to spend their future not only helping others, but to bring happiness to each other.

The phone calls started coming. It seemed that everyone knew that Del and Patti would soon be moving. First one person and then another invited them to come live at their home.

All were thanked for their invitations, but told that this young couple now planned to get an apartment of their own.

10

Just a Little Thing?

"Please come see me before I leave." Del heard his brother's voice on the telephone. "They plan to ship us out to Korea in two or three weeks."

"How can we do it, Patti? I can't get off work, and besides, there is no money for gas."

Patti looked into her husband's troubled eyes. "We'll do it, Honey. Orvin may never come back. We will do it."

Del looked so tired. His afternoon job as sawyer at Hazelton sawmill in Walla Walla lasted late into the night. Still, the college expenses always devoured most of his paycheck. There was little left for luxuries such as gas and tires for the car.

Patti wrapped her arms around her husband. "We can leave Friday after your classes. Then we will drive home Saturday night. We must go."

Darkness covered the land by the time Del and Patti arrived in Fort Lewis, Washington, that Friday evening and finally found the room where Doris and Orvin, with their baby girl, were staying.

As Patti sat and listened to Doris tell what it was like to be left with a small child, and a car she hardly knew how to drive when Orvin had been transferred from Texas to the Northwest, Patti knew God had given Doris extra strength. Doris' sister had flown from Oregon to help take care of little Dianne and help Doris drive to the West Coast. They had packed a lunch for the first day and stopped at a rest area to eat. Doris' purse fell out of the car and lay beside the road. They ate their lunch and again started on the long drive to Washington, never dreaming they were leaving Doris' purse, containing all of her money behind.

When the ladies stopped for the night they discovered that Doris' purse was missing. Her sister counted out most of the money she had with her and paid for the motel room.

What should they do? What could they do? They prayed, earnestly pleading with God to help them get the purse back from wherever it happened to be. Doris called the police. She gave them the details and prayed for guidance. The next morning Doris called the police again. Had they heard anything about her missing purse? God was already answering their prayers. The purse was on the bus coming to her. She could pick it up that afternoon. Someone had found the purse lying beside the road and took it to the police station.

"It was all there! All the money and everything else still in the purse!" Doris' eyes sparkled. "I think God used something as little as a purse to let us know He is in charge and hasn't forgotten us." A sweet peace covered Doris' countenance.

Del and Patti said "goodbye" long after they had planned to leave. It was hard to pull away and head for home. Darkness and fog covered the city by the time they got into their car and started down the road. Del strained his eyes to see the yellow line. The fog had moved in to such an extent that Patti stuck her head out the window as they inched along— and told Del when the car got too close to the edge of the road.

Thank You, God, for giving encouragement to Doris, Patti conversed with her Friend, *but sometimes You seem so far away. There never seems to be any time to do anything fun and no money anyway. I realize I shouldn't be discouraged, but would You please show me You are in charge of our lives, too? Maybe in just some little thing please let me know?*

The hours slowly passed. The fog continued to lay heavy without a break until Patti wondered if this trip had been another mistake. When the fog finally began to clear, Del parked the car on the side of the road.

"You will have to drive," he mumbled. "I can't stay awake a minute longer."

He laid his head back; sleep took possession of him before Patti had time to adjust the seat and start the motor.

"Let's see—where did I put my little purse?" She turned on the dome light.

"Del, could you hand me my purse?"

Del awoke and looked around. "What do you need your purse for?"

"I don't know. I just want to know where it is."

"Hey, it's here some place." He looked around again. "I can't find it. Let's go or we will never get home in time."

"If it is here, please hand it to me."

"What do you need it for?"

"I don't know. I feel I must have it."

By this time sleep had fled and exasperation had taken its place while Del checked everywhere for Patti's purse.

"Let's go." Del spoke as though that settled the matter. Lying back he closed his eyes. Patti could hear his deep breathing.

11

To Have and To Hold

"Del, I can't find my purse. Please just open the door and check beside the road."

"Why?" Then he swung the door open and caught his breath. He slipped from the car and came back holding Patti's purse.

"You must have dropped your purse out of the car when you went around to the driver's side. How did you know it wasn't in the car?"

"I didn't. I just had a strong urgency to find it before driving on."

Tears of happiness made little paths down Patti's cheeks while she drove and Del slept. *Dear Lord, how could I have even questioned Your love?* She spoke to her Friend. *Why did I even need this special token of Your leading, God?* "And ye shall seek Me, and find Me, when ye shall search for Me with all your heart." —Jeremiah 29:13. She breathed a happy sigh. "Thank You. Thank You, God."

Hazel, Patti's wonderful friend from the G & D Insurance Company, had helped Patti find a daylight basement apartment that she and Del liked. They now also owned a big freezer. She preserved all the food she could. Berries, corn, and any other fruits and vegetables she found went into the freezer.

Hazel and her husband had a beautiful little three-year-old daughter and were expecting another baby in a few months. "When are you and Del going to have a family?" Hazel had come over to Patti's apartment to help her do some painting.

"Del and I don't plan to have any children until he finishes college. I need to work a few more years after that, too."

Hazel laughed. "You remind me of that poem written by Richard Armour. Have you ever heard the poem *To Have and Too Old*?"

"No."

"Well that is what you remind me of. Oh, let me see. How does that go? Now I remember—

> *The bride, white of hair, is stooped over her cane,*
> *Her faltering footsteps need guiding*
> *While down the church aisle with wan toothless smile,*
> *The groom in a wheelchair is riding.*
> *And who is this elderly couple you ask?*
> *You'll find, when you closely explain it,*
> *That here is the rare, most conservative pair*
> *Who waited till they could afford it.*

"If you wait to have children until you can afford them, you will be too old to have any."

"I doubt that." Patti giggled.

"That is true." Hazel looked serious. "If you wait until you really want them, you will want them so badly you can't have any."

A good friend like Hazel might be right. Why do I want to keep working anyway?

When school started that fall, food filled every space in the freezer. There was money for Del's college entrance fee. Most important of all, Del and Patti were eagerly looking forward to the arrival of their new baby.

Mother Wagner's sister, Dr. Laura Miller, was Patti's physician. Patti learned to love Aunt Laura as the months passed and her little "somebody" grew. At two-thirty one frosty, clear, morning, while the stars shone brightly and the countryside slept, Del called Aunt Laura. "I am taking Patti to the hospital," he told her.

After asking some questions, Aunt Laura said, "Del, go ahead and take Patti to the hospital. I will call the best doctor in town. I have had a heart attack, so I cannot go. She will be in good hands. Dr. Hammer is an excellent doctor."

A heart attack! Not Aunt Laura, the best doctor in town! Aunt Laura, who had graduated from Loma Linda third highest in her class, and then humbly given her life for others, had had a heart attack!

"Oh, Del, what shall we do?" Patti thought her heart would break.

"Go to the hospital." He picked up the suitcase.

"But I mean Aunt Laura. Where is she?"

"At home. I just talked to her. Is this suitcase all you need to take?"

"Yes."

"Then let's go." Del held the door open.

That evening in the hospital Patti could hardly believe so many people would come with flowers, plants and cards. It seemed like a party. Del had never looked so proud. He must have told the world about his new son, Edward Duane.

Two months after Eddie's birth, Del graduated from Walla Walla College, and the place rang with laughter as relatives and friends came to celebrate and attend his graduation. Patti sat in the audience this day—this golden day of spring—and watched her husband get his college diploma.

After the ceremony, he handed his diploma to her. "You

may have this." Tenderly he reached out and took Eddie. Love and commitment showed on the face of this young father, and he smiled as he looked into the eyes of his tiny son.

Held in the arms of a devoted father, Eddie smiled back, never imagining the power he possessed—in the highest conceivable degree—to bring joy and undreamed of fear into the heart of his mother.

12

In Business

Sawmill work flowed in Del's blood, and by 1956 with college classes and tuition bills all history, he was starting a profitable business for himself—or so he thought. Del had bought a portable sawmill and had it hauled up into the Wallowa Mountains where there was a stretch of timber that needed to be cut. He now owned his own sawmill and hired his own crew. Ken, a new acquaintance, was in charge of the logging operation.

Del was very excited, so early one morning Del, Patti and Eddie left College Place where they lived, to go to Palmer Junction, north of Elgin, on an adventure of finding a house to live somewhere close to the new sawmill. Del had already talked to two different people who had places they said could be fixed up for occupancy. He had not looked at them yet, but wanted Patti to go with him to choose where she wanted to live.

From the main road the first place looked like a cute little log cabin, located on a hill overlooking the valley below. It sat there snuggled under big trees. Patti's heart pounded as they started up the long, narrow driveway. It looked so cute, but oh, dear. She would be just too far from any neighbors. That part about it she didn't like. The closer they came to the cabin the worse it looked. Instead of a cute little cabin as it appeared from the road, it was an old broken-down log cabin trying to keep from falling apart. The front door hung open by one hinge. As she and Del went into the building through the front door, a herd of goats rushed out the back door. It looked as if the goats had been using the building as an outhouse for many years.

"Let's see what the other place looks like." Del headed the car down the long driveway. The next place appeared to have been built for storage, and that is what it was being used for. However, it had been fixed up for people to live in at one time, and recently the people who owned the place had cleaned it up and moved the sacks of grain from where they had been in the building. There was a bedroom with an old bedstead in it, a kitchen with a table, a couple of chairs, and an old wood-stove to cook on. They wouldn't try to use the living room because that is where the sacks of grain had been moved. There was a well, the windows had glass in them, and the doors shut. The other advantage was it was close to the bottom of the mountain where Del would be working every day.

The car had been traded in for a truck, so that Del would have a vehicle to carry the equipment needed for the logging operation. This was loaded with some of their personal belongings, and Del, Patti, and Eddie made the journey to the shed-house at the bottom of the mountain. After unloading their things, Del had brought in water and did what he could to make his family comfortable. Before leaving for the mountains he said, "Be sure to boil the water very well before using it." Then he was gone.

Patti walked around inspecting her new home. *Well, I had better get busy. Eddie is nearly out of formula and I must get this water boiled so it will have time to cool before his next feeding time.* She built up the fire, put water in a kettle, and set it on the stove. There was a crack that ran across the top of the stove, making a sort of a bulge where the crack didn't fit together and kept the water from boiling. Patti kept putting more and more wood into the stove, but the water still wouldn't boil!!

After Eddie had finished the formula she had brought from home and gone to sleep, she walked outside and looked for the pump to get more water. The pump didn't work. *How had Del gotten the water? Oh, dear what should she do?* She raised a few boards and looked down. There was the water—and—and—something was swimming around in it! Horror shot through her body and came to rest in the pit of her stomach. She would never think of letting her baby drink that water no matter how long it boiled, but it wouldn't even boil!!! *Surely Del had not seen that snake.* She slammed down the boards and rushed back into the building.

Hours later, Del walked into the house and found two people in tears. He gathered them in his arms and anxiously inquired what the trouble had been. Patti laid her head on his shoulder and began sobbing out her pitiful story. But before the long, sad narrative of the day had ended, Del, being a man of action, had their things picked up and packed into the truck. Then, the loaded truck headed back over the mountains to College Place.

Patti had already made up her mind what she was going to do. A little over a year ago, she had finally gotten a job at the Corps of Engineers. She never did pass the shorthand test, but came so close to passing, the fellow said he felt sure she could do the work. She just wouldn't be getting paid as much as if she had reached the next test level for the government.

Working for three men, each wanting his work done first, became a challenge. The head man in Patti's division had a big office next to her room, with a little opening where he could shove his work onto her desk. He smoked continually, and when he had a conference meeting most of the men were smoking—with the smoke making its way into her office.

This had been a few months before Eddie was born, and the smoke didn't help her feel any better. With a heavy heart she told her boss that she must resign. The man in charge of hiring new employees had told her, "If you ever need a job, there will be one here for you."

That had been nearly a year ago, but now Patti knew exactly what she planned to do. She'd find someone to take care of Eddie and then go back to get a job at the Corps of Engineers while Del worked on the mountain. They could be together on weekends.

A few days later Mother Wagner came to visit. After listening to Patti for awhile she went outside where Del was working to talk with him. He came inside radiant with excitement, and said, "You know Mother has just gotten a nice little trailer house to live in while she teaches school in Vale. She has offered to loan it to us until we can find somewhere suitable to live. We will haul it up to the mountaintop and can live right by my work. She will rent an apartment until we don't need it anymore. Isn't that wonderful?"

Patti loved the beautiful mountains, and now she would be right by Del all day. He could even come home for lunch. With a grateful heart, Del hauled the neat, little home up the winding mountain road and parked it a short distance from the portable sawmill. Mother Wagner came to see that they were nicely settled before she left to find an apartment in Vale, Oregon.

Patti's heart burst with happiness as she stood at the door of the comfortable little dwelling and looked for miles down into the valley below. The cool air caressed tall pine trees with a gentle breeze. What a beautiful place to live, in these Wallowa Mountains in northeast Oregon. She glanced at her precious baby asleep in his basket and grabbed an empty bucket. Slipping out of the mobile she rushed down the steep mountain to a small spring. Then she hung the bucket over a pipe someone had stuck into the side of the mountain, and rested while the bucket filled with cool, clear water. When the bucket was full she hurried up the steep mountain path as fast as she could. *What if Eddie woke up while she was gone?*

There were always diapers to wash, so there was always a need to carry water. Patti saw deer, elk, and the tracks of other animals that came to drink down at the little stream as it went singing away through the forest. The scent of the pine filled the air. She thanked God for the strength to be like the pioneer women who built this country in the West.

Patti appreciated getting back to their College Place apartment on the weekends whenever they could. At the apartment she enjoyed the luxury of washing all of their clothes in a washing machine and soaking herself in the bathtub. Eddie was the only one who got a decent bath every day up in the mountains. Del would come in so covered with dirt and sawdust, Patti would tell him that the only thing she recognized was his eyes. But he enjoyed every minute of it. He loved seeing the big logs pulled in by the caterpillar and watching the loads of lumber roar down the road. He worked as hard and as long hours as before, and she realized that was just Del.

Whenever a truckload of lumber passed, it rolled up great clouds of dust and scattered them over everything in the vicinity. Patti kept going farther and farther back into the woods to hang Eddie's freshly washed diapers on the trees to keep them from being covered with the ever-present dust. When the diapers were dry, she would gather the squares of white flannel and fold them carefully so they were just the right size. Then she put them in the box under the bed with the rest of Eddie's clean clothes.

Before going back down the mountain, she used the big bowl as a bathtub and put on clean clothes. Still, she always felt grimy by the time she got to town. There was no way to keep out the dust that would roll in from somewhere whenever they traveled down the logging road. Going to the little town of Elgin with Del and another man, she glanced at the sawdust sticking out of the man's ears. *Should I tell him? Would he be embarrassed? Why bother? This sawmill work has become such a part of them it is sticking out of their ears!*

13

Nearly Lost

Sunday morning arrived. It was time to head back to the mountains from their comfortable College Place apartment.

"I can get a ride back up to the logging site with some of the fellows." Del smiled at Patti. "Why don't you stay here, Honey, and enjoy the apartment for a few days? Gary said the part for the mill will be ready Wednesday. You can bring it up in the truck."

She looked at the sky. Autumn had held her ground, but winter scowled at the delay. *What if it started storming?*

On Wednesday, with the part repaired, Patti gathered her things and put them into the truck. She filled the floor in front of the seat with boxes of clean clothes. Eddie's basket occupied most of the seat beside her. Then she filled the empty spaces with food to take to the logging site. She placed Eddie in his little bed, and headed out to be with her husband again.

When Patti's truck started up the mountains, she noticed that it had begun snowing. At first the flakes were only here and there, but soon the snow became thicker. She could hardly see where the road ended and the canyon began. She continued praying with wide open eyes, but the snowflakes coming at her onto the windshield made the whole world feel as if it was swirling with the wind and snow. *Please, God, what shall I do?* The truck moved forward slowly, but *where was it going?* She thought of her little son lying so quietly beside her. She thought of the wilderness all around.

A little while before, the country had been calm and green under a cold gray sky, and now the air was filled with pelting snow that drove with fury and whirled in a biting wind. Patti strained her eyes. *Should I stop? Should I keep going? Help! God. Help! Guide me through this awful storm. What should I do? Oh, what* should *I do?* She was afraid to keep going. She was afraid to stop.

Patti continued driving through the frightful blizzard. *What was that?* She thought she could see a faint shadow of something moving in front of her. At first she could not make out what it might be—only a blur through the bank of white. *Oh, it's a snowplow! Thank You. Thank You, God.* Now she could just follow the snowplow. The snow continued blowing in waves. Sometimes she had clear vision and sometimes blurred, but the lights of the plow were like beacons to keep Patti on the road.

She dare not take her eyes from the road but reached over to feel her precious baby. She felt no movement and his little hands were ice cold. *Oh, God! My baby! My baby!* Everything looked so white except that snowplow in front of the truck. That snowplow was making it possible for her to keep going. It felt chilly in the truck. Patti had covered Eddie well. She must not panic. Her job was to keep this truck on the road headed for the little town of Elgin. Mile after mile she drove. She had never prayed harder in her whole life. *Why had Eddie's hands turned so cold?* Icy fingers of fear clutched at her heart.

When Patti felt it safe, she parked the truck and checked to see what she could do for her young son. Eddie looked up at her with those trusting eyes and smiled into her face. She took her baby in her arms and hugged him to her heart. As she did so, a bag of frozen corn fell from the blanket.

"Oh, Eddie, how did you ever reach those frozen vegetables?"

With a song in her heart and praise on her lips to her Heavenly Father, she drove through the little town of Elgin, past the houses at Palmer Junction, and up the steep winding logging road.

"Let me see—oh, dear, which road did Daddy tell Mama not to take?" Patti smiled at Eddie as she continued talking to the little boy sitting up in his basket playing with a fuzzy white bear.

"I think I am supposed to keep to the right, and then turn to the left at a 'V'. Oh, dear. This is hard to remember with all the new roads the men have been creating lately."

Eddie turned his little head toward her. His eyes were big with confidence. He did not seem one bit worried about getting lost. *Oh, for the faith of a little child. Please God, my Heavenly Father, help me to always trust You with childlike faith like Eddie trusts us.* She would soon be to her little home and husband. Patti's heart was full of thankfulness to have arrived safely and happiness overflowed her very being—until—

Del was not there! Something was wrong! She could not hear the whine of the sawmill, and no one was around. She stacked the frozen food in the ice box; she changed and fed Eddie. Heating a bowl of soup and cutting a slice of bread that she had baked the day before, she picked Eddie up and talked to him as she waited, and waited, and waited.

Where was everybody? What had happened? The place felt lonely, cold, and isolated. Usually she could hear the caterpillar or chain saws running. Now everything was so quiet. Winter was coming, so Del had kept things going as fast as he could.

Some of the men had sold Del on the idea that they could run the little sawmill all winter. Patti did not want to be here in the winter. She could not even imagine living up here in all the ice and snow. *What if they got hungry, sick, or hurt?* Del convinced her they had this portable sawmill to pay for. It must be kept going as long as possible.

Patti held Eddie close to her heart as she peered out the window and prayed. She was miles from anyone. This was not a good place to be. *Oh, God what shall I do?*

"Trust in the Lord with all thine heart; and lean not unto thine own understanding. In all thy ways acknowledge Him, and He shall direct thy paths" (Proverbs 3: 5, 6).

"Oh, thank You, God, for Your love and guidance. Please send Del home soon. Please help that no one was hurt or killed. Help me to trust in You with all my heart and not lean to my own understanding. These things I ask in the name of Jesus. Amen."

Time stood still before she heard the rumble of someone's truck coming up the mountain road. She saw it stop and Del get out before it turned and headed back down the mountain.

"Del! Del!" Patti rushed into his arms. He held her close and said, "We're finished. Ken got mad at the loggers and fired them. He didn't have the money to pay them, so they tied up every log in the woods. We have nothing to saw."

He dropped to a chair like a limb falling from a tree. He had put so much into this project; now it was all over. They sat a long time quietly talking and thinking. Then Del stood. He looked around the place. "We might as well move out." A look of determination and courage returned to his face. "We need to get this trailer house off the mountain while the weather will still let us."

What a man! Patti knew Del was extremely disappointed,

but ready to rise to the occasion. Her heart overflowed with relief, gratitude, and wonder. Silently she thanked her God that they would not be living on the mountain that winter.

She had already felt winter's icy fingers. The economy had shut down several mills, throwing men out of work. *How would they pay the bills this business had already stacked up for them?* Patti shook herself. *Why am I worrying? God just answered my plea to Him that we wouldn't have to live here this winter. What a God!!! Now I will wait and see how He plans to work this problem out.*

14

Poverty, Or Is It Riches?

"Where will you find a job, Del?"

Mother Wagner's mobile home had been moved to Vale, Oregon, where she had rented an apartment and was teaching school.

"Don't worry. I can always find something." Del defied the statements of his unemployed friends who said that there were no jobs available. Those friends had not inquired at the State Mental Hospital in Pendleton, Oregon. Patti marveled at Del's ability to work at anything that needed to be done. He didn't stop looking for another job, but this would keep them in groceries and pay the rent.

Patti was looking for a job as well. Annabelle, a lady Patti had gotten acquainted with a short time before, seemed nice and would take care of Eddie. After the first day out searching for employment, Patti came back to pick up Eddie and heard him screaming before she even got to the front door.

What could be wrong? She had never heard Eddie scream like that. She practically flew up the steps and banged on the door. Annabelle called, "Come in," and Patti rushed to the bedroom where Annabelle was changing a wet diaper. She picked up her sobbing son and gathered up the diaper bag with only one sopping diaper in it—the one that had just been taken off Eddie.

With trembling heart, she paid Annabelle and told her she probably wasn't going to get a job right away. Then she and Eddie sobbed most of the way back to the little two-room basement apartment located behind the utility room in an elderly lady's home.

This apartment was not like the daylight basement apartment they were still renting at College Place that looked out over a large green lawn and down to the valley below. This apartment was only temporary and was the cheapest thing they could find in the better—well at least not the worst—part of town. It wasn't fun living there, but they usually went back to College Place on the weekends.

The next morning Patti washed her hair and rolled it in huge rollers. She also did the washing and hung the clothes on the lines across the utility room—the room they had to go through to come inside. Eddie was crawling around on the floor, and Patti heard a knock. It wasn't on her door, but on the outside door leading into the utility room. She went to answer it.

The young assistant pastor from the Pendleton Church stood waiting at the door dressed in a dark suit, white shirt and tie. She and Del had attended that church a couple of times, and now the pastor had come by to encourage them to come back. She invited him in, and maneuvering their way through the wet sheets, diapers, and other clothes hanging on the lines, they came to her front door, which was really their only door, and it went right into the kitchen. The pastor sat on one of the two old kitchen chairs in the room while Patti picked Eddie up off the floor and sat on the other old chair.

After long moments of strained conversation while the

young man studied the interior of the dingy little room, he excused himself because he had "other calls to make." Patti led the way back out to the door through the hanging wet socks, shirts, pants and underclothes. She had been washing clothes all morning, and the clotheslines were loaded to capacity.

I hope he encourages the other people he is going to visit. He certainly didn't encourage me! Patti felt demoralized. It seemed that this young man had been a long way removed from his comfort zone while visiting in her home. She had felt his pity, his arrogance—*or was it disdain?* He had tried to say the correct things. She could tell that, but with an attitude of condescension, what did he plan to accomplish? Where was the humility of Christ?

Then a wave of anger moved through her veins. *It isn't fair the way poor people get looked down on!! I look very poor, and I am—well, at least financially right now, but I am the same person I was when we lived at F.W. Peterson's place. That pastor would have treated me much differently if I had answered the door at the Peterson's residence.*

"Oh, God, help me to see people through Your eyes. Poverty, riches, education, power or prestige means nothing to You." Patti was talking to her best Friend. Then as an afterthought she added, "Please help that man. It seems to me he has so much to learn before he can be a success in Your work."

A few days later Del came home, picked up Eddie and gathered Patti in his arms. "How would you like to move back to central Oregon?"

15

Home Again

"How would you like to move back to central Oregon?" Del tried to look sober, but his eyes were smiling.

"Oh, Del—really?" He held Patti close while tears of joy streamed down her face. This was better than she could ask or think. She loved beautiful central Oregon, her home country where she had lived since she was ten years old. Now they were moving back.

They loaded up their things from the apartment and were soon driving to Patti's parent's place. It was a wonderful reunion. Then after a couple of days or so, Del and her Dad climbed into his big farm truck and headed for College Place to move all of their things from the apartment there.

Del and Patti looked at places for rent around Redmond and Bend for a few days, but everything seemed too expensive to a couple of young people who were planning to work and pay off all the bills the business had stacked up that summer. They chose to live by her parent's home on the farm. Their residence would be a little building that had originally been built for the chickens, but no chicken had lived in it for years. To most people it would be just a little farm building, but to her it was a part of the past, a step to the future, and a home for the present. Patti's dad and Del worked at remodeling the little building, while she and her family lived in the farmhouse with her folks.

Del's mother, the energetic little lady that she was, came to visit for a few days. She built a closet in the bedroom which also worked as a wall for the nursery. She must have measured precisely, for the little room on the other side of the closet was exactly the right size to squeeze a crib into. New blue wallpaper with little animals all over it completed Eddie's room. Patti continued to live in a world of surprise seeing all the things Mother Wagner could do.

Del laughed. "You didn't know she helped build the house that I grew up in?" Patti knew Mother Wagner had taught school and raised three children by herself after Del's father had been killed by a speeding car, but she did not know Mother Wagner was also a carpenter.

The carpet remnant she bought worked well for wall to wall carpeting in the front room. New wallpaper and paint helped to compensate for the many other things the house lacked. Patti bought dark green material that looked nice with the freshly-painted floor and created curtains to hang over the shelves Del made in the kitchen. She found frilly, white curtains to fit the kitchen and front room windows. The curtains for the bedroom she tailored so they could be drawn like drapes at night.

Del hooked a hose to a water faucet by the farmhouse and buried it under the driveway. It worked well bringing water into the little kitchen if the weather was neither too hot—when the plastic hose would swell and had to be turned off to keep it from breaking—or too cold—when the water froze.

Del was busily working at a lumber mill and molding plant in Redmond. His paycheck from Whittier Molding would go to pay bills—all of it, after the tithe and offerings were taken out. Patti found a job a few weeks later. Her paycheck from her secretarial job at Mann Construction paid current expenses. Eddie thrived on his grandparent's loving care while his mommy and daddy were working full-time jobs. The little portable sawmill had been sold to someone who wanted it worse than either Del or Patti did. By living in the small house and being careful, Del and Patti were soon able to pay off all the bills from the year before.

It wasn't fun when some of Patti's friends would come over to visit and not be able to understand why they were living in such a small house or why Del worked at what appeared to be a mediocre job.

"A college graduate and working in a lumber mill?" Alice repeated her words over and over. It wasn't that she just bugged Patti about it, but she talked about it to everyone. "Did you know Del graduated from college and is just working in a lumber mill? It takes thousands of dollars to go to college. Anyone can work in a lumber mill."

Alice and her family had watched Patti and Del struggle through college. These had been her friends, friends who had not gone to college, but had kept busy doing fun things while she and Del sacrificed pleasure for good grades.

After a while Patti had had enough.

"Of course Del has a college education," she stormed, "but he is **man enough** not to let it ruin him. He doesn't consider himself too good to work at whatever is available.

If he did, his college education would be a detriment to him. It would be like stuffing him in a box where he wouldn't do things he is capable of doing."

No one could put Del in a box. He rarely slowed his break-neck pace. Even at the mill he continually learned new skills. Soon he was doing the electrical work and also working with the owners on new projects. Before long, Del's main work consisted in making devices to improve production, helping design new equipment, and also spending hours seeing how it could be done electronically.

Little did anyone know at that time, that the experiences Del was having working in the lumber industry would lead him to invent equipment that would not only change the industry, but would also bring in an income which would sustain the family for years to come.

He went to night school and stayed at the top of his class as an electronic engineer technician while working full time and doing a little business on his own.

In the meantime, Patti had quit her job, and Del had built another room onto their postage-stamp sized house. In it they put a new little crib and a chest of drawers.

A cold January had welcomed in the year 1958 with ice and snow. The media said another storm was approaching.

"I think I had better go to Redmond and get four new snow tires on the car." Patti's dad was sharing his concern with her mother. "I am going to keep the car filled with gas. Who knows when Del and Patti's new baby will arrive!"

Not more than two days later an ice storm arrived covering the trees and all roads with thick ice. That was the morning little Judy decided it was time to see the outside world.

Patti knew it was God who had impressed her father to get new snow tires on the car as they slowly crawled the five and a half miles to the Redmond Hospital over the treacherous roads. The nurse on duty gave Patti a shot trying to slow things down so the doctor could get there in time. After a few days in the hospital, with bells ringing in their hearts, Del and Patti brought little Judy home and introduced her to Eddie.

The weather continued to be windy and cold. Patti became housebound. Whenever she tried to take Judy anyplace, Judy would get wind colic; and Patti would be up most of the night rocking the little baby.

When Judy was about five weeks old, Patti and her mother decided to go to a baby shower for a friend. It was fun to get out of the house and do something special. Del and her dad were sure they would be able to take care of Eddie and little Judy. However, about an hour after the party started, the telephone rang. It was for Patti. Del seemed alarmed. "Judy has been crying ever since you left. We can't seem to do anything to get her to quit. I think you had better come home."

Patti and her mother left the party and hurried home. When they arrived, they found Del and Patti's dad happily visiting. Both children were fast asleep.

16

"No, God, No"

With a sigh of relief, Patti dropped into the nearest chair. At last! Eddie and Judy were sleeping. It would help if Del could be home evenings once in awhile to help with these little people whose energy increased as the day wore on and Patti wore out. Well, there was no reason to even think about it, for he started work at seven in the morning and then went straight to classes at Bend Community College. He usually did not get home until ten or eleven at night.

Patti heard the back door of her parent's home shut. Soon her father was quietly knocking on the door of her tiny home.

"You are wanted on the phone," he whispered. "I will wait over here while you answer it."

"Oh, Patti, I had forgotten you didn't have a phone at your place." Juanita, the pastor's wife was on the line. "I would never have called so late, but I really need your help."

A few months before, Juanita had been in a bad car accident. The car was demolished, and Juanita had suffered injuries. The recuperation was slow and painful.

"It is this way," Juanita sighed. "I don't know what to do, and I have to have some answers. You know I was planning to lead in Vacation Bible School before the accident. I am not sure that I can do it now. Ethel said if I will just lead this year, she will do it after that, but I am the only one who knows how, and someone has to get Vacation Bible School (VBS) started here."

"I see." Patti was sympathetic, but quite relieved that they probably would not be having VBS this year. She secretly feared Juanita would be expecting everyone in the little church to help.

"Last night," Juanita continued, "I had decided to pray this thing through and not stop until God impressed me what He wanted. I don't know how long I prayed, but I fell asleep on my knees, and when I awoke I felt so cold. My only impression was to get back into bed and get warm. Now I don't know why God doesn't seem to answer, but I must know what to do. It would be better not to start Vacation Bible School than to start and not be able to finish, so I am asking a favor of you. Would you pray and ask God what we should do about Vacation Bible School?"

"Of course."

Patti's heart was light as she quickly went to see if the children were still sleeping and give her dad a chance to get back home. She did not feel tired or a bit discouraged anymore. How fortunate they were to have the Kretschmars, a pastor and wife who worked so close to the Lord, as friends.

Joyfully she knelt in the little space between the bed and dresser and thanked God for His many blessings. *I must not forget Juanita's request, but it seems almost like presumption to expect God to tell me what He wants to do about VBS when Juanita has not received an answer. Surely God does not expect Juanita to try to do so much after the terrible accident she has been in. No, there will not be Vacation Bible School this year. I am thankful for that. Why is everyone pushing so hard to have it anyway? Well, a promise is a promise.*

Patti had told Juanita she would pray about it, and she did mention it to God before rising from her knees. The answer came so fast it hit like a bolt of lightning. Her mouth went dry, and her heart pounded. She felt weak all over. The voice in her thoughts said, "You must tell Juanita to have Vacation Bible School, and you, Patti, will help in any way that is needed."

"Oh, no, God, I can't do that."

Then the awful realization of what she had just told God struck her. "I am not telling You 'no,' God. I will never do that. It is just—I am incapable."

"Who made your mouth?" The voice in her thoughts came suddenly, but very clear.

Patti prayed many times during the next few days and weeks, always telling God that she would never tell Him "no" but putting off what He had told her to do.

Gradually the conviction left her and so did her peace and closeness to God. Her days were filled with activity, and finally she forgot all about Vacation Bible School—until—with a full dosage of remorse sweeping over her, she listened as Juanita explained that she really did not know what to do, but had decided to go ahead with VBS. At this point Patti courageously said she felt that was the right thing to do.

Then Juanita continued, "I want you to be junior leader."

17

Vacation Bible School

Juanita, the pastor's wife, had just asked Patti to be junior leader for Vacation Bible School. Doesn't Juanita know I cannot be junior leader? Doesn't she know I have never done anything like that in my life? Of course she is only kidding. Juanita is so much fun!!

"I will do anything I can to help." *That is what God told me to say. Thank You, God, for working this out, and please forgive me.* Patti took a deep breath. Already a burden was being lifted from her shoulders as she accepted the responsibility. They would have VBS, and she would do anything she could do to help like assist in registration or even on the playground.

"I will help in any way I can, Juanita, but we must have someone who is good and with experience to do the junior division. Of course I will do whatever you need."

"Thanks." Juanita looked happy.

The weeks flew by. Juanita said no more about VBS. Patti was relieved and happy since Juanita must have taken her advice and gotten someone good who had been a junior leader and knew what to do. Sometimes she had a fleeting thought wondering why Juanita never mentioned that she should be an assistant or anything, but that was fine. She wasn't about to rock the boat.

When the announcement was made in church one Sabbath morning that all those helping with the new Vacation Bible School outreach program should meet at the pastor's home the next Thursday evening at seven o'clock, Patti decided to go. The ladies were there with stacks of material and last minute questions. Everyone seemed busy and organized. Then someone asked who the junior leader was.

"Patti is." Juanita continued to answer questions and organize the group.

Patti? Junior leader? Then Juanita wasn't kidding! She really does expect me to be junior leader!! Why hadn't Juanita talked to me about it besides that one evening? Patti knew in her heart it was her own fault. She had no idea what happened during the rest of that meeting. One thing she knew— she was tired of arguing with God.

After the meeting, she waited until everyone had gone before talking to Juanita. Patti knew Juanita had used all the strength she had just to hold the meeting and did not need any more frustrations.

"You know, Juanita, I would rather have the kindergarten class than the juniors."

Juanita looked at Patti in utter astonishment. "You can't have the kindergarten! Ethel is taking that. She has been working on it for weeks."

Still very much aware that she came to help and not be a burden, Patti answered, "Then I need to know what it is all about."

Again she got this look of absolute unbelief.

"I-I-I mean." Patti looked around the room. "Don't you have some guides or literature or something for me to study?"

"But I gave those to you weeks ago." Juanita had this same look of total astonishment.

Now Patti became positive. "No, I really haven't received

anything." Her mind was in a whirl, but that was one thing she did know.

"Really?" Juanita went to look in her cupboard where she kept her VBS material.

"It is not here." She stood a moment, thinking. "Oh, I remember. You were gone that day I was visiting all my leaders, so I just laid the material on your couch. I left it there, Patti, so you just have to have it."

"Okay, I will check." She hurried to the car. Panic cut through Patti like a knife. There was no other junior leader. It was completely up to her, and she had no idea what it was all about!! Juanita thought she had been studying the material, but she had never even seen it. Well, there was no reason to let Juanita know how desperate she felt. Arriving home, she frantically searched the house, but found nothing. Then she went to get the children and asked her mother if she had seen the VBS material. Her mother had not seen it. When Del came in from class that evening, she asked him if he had seen the VBS material.

"I really don't think so." He started getting ready for bed.

"Oh, Del!" The tears flooded Patti's face. "Juanita brought all this material over and left it on the couch, and I have never even seen it!"

"Oh. That was weeks ago. I came home from work on a Friday. You were gone, and all this stuff lay all over the couch, so I just gathered it all up and put it away."

"Where?"

"Up on that top shelf."

On a shelf so high it was never used sat stacks of VBS material for juniors. There were crafts to be done, workbooks, and instruction books for the leaders.

All of this to do in just two days! Patti spent a lot of time Friday praying and trying to figure out how to motivate their own juniors to be good hosts at VBS.

Sabbath Patti spoke to the juniors in their Sabbath School class. Most of the juniors coming to VBS would be from the community, and she wanted the juniors from her church to realize the responsibility they had and the important part they would be having in this undertaking. These kids were really great, but there were also problems, and no one seemed to be able to understand how to handle them. Two junior leaders had already resigned that year. They were conscientious leaders, but neither felt they could handle the confusion the lively juniors created each week.

With all of that going on, Patti absolutely couldn't believe Juanita actually expected her to lead the junior division at VBS.

Five-month-old Judy got fussy during the church service, and since there was no mother's room in the small church, Patti took Judy outside for a little stroll in the beautiful sunshine. She noticed Tom*, the biggest and oldest boy from the junior division, and Timmy**, one of the littler kids also outside. Tom was teasing Timmy and giving him a bad time. Timmy was getting mad. Timmy was known for his anger, and Patti didn't blame him. She would be angry, too, if she were being treated that way. She was ready to walk over and talk with the two boys, but by now church had just gotten out and Tom walked back to the crowd of people. Timmy was so angry by this time he ran up behind Tom and hit him on the back as hard as he could. People looked aghast, and Tom just grabbed Timmy's hands and told him very kindly, but loud enough so everyone could hear, that that was not the way to act at church. He should be nice to people, etc. etc.

Wow! Tom sure knows how to make the adults think he is a

---

*   Name has been changed
**   Name has been changed

wonderful guy. Even Juanita depended a lot on Tom and had told Patti that morning she had asked him, Tom, to be Patti's special helper. "He is big, and the kids seem to respect him." Juanita looked pleased.

"You won't need to be responsible during break. I have asked Tom to be in charge of the games."

Sunday Patti started working on the program. Thank God for her mother who not only took care of the children but also filled in by preparing the meals for the family.

The local paper and radio had informed the community that the children who lived in Terrebonne and wished to be a part of the VBS activities—if they needed transportation—they should meet at the Post Office before 8:30 Monday morning. Monday morning came in like a whirl. When Patti got to the Post Office, the station wagon driven by another VBS leader was already loaded to capacity. Still, ten or eleven little children waited in line. This was before seat belts and restrictions, so the rest of the children squeezed into the car Patti had borrowed from her parents. The children were practically hanging out the windows as Patti drove the five miles to the church in Redmond. She hardly heard the happy voices of the wound up children packed around her.

"*Oh, God,*" Patti pleaded, "*please remember whose idea it was in the first place that I do this. It is up to You.*" She laughed and visited with the joyful group, but most of the time she was really pleading with God for His help and wisdom.

At the church she helped the children get registered before they entered the church for a general assembly. Tom played the trumpet to get everyone's attention. Then came a special welcome and announcements before enlivening songs, a devotion, and prayer. Next the children separated going to their different divisions.

The junior room was packed to capacity as the energized juniors filled every chair available. Patti spoke a few minutes, and soon they were listening with undivided attention as she presented the lesson for that day—and—then—suddenly—a loud commotion broke out in the back of the room.

18

The Problem

What was happening? Patti read questioning, shocked expressions on the faces before her. Immediately Tom was at his job taking care of the emergency. He told the kids to be quiet and motioned for them to pay attention to the teacher. Soon everything was back to normal. The rest of the day turned out great. Patti loved the juniors. What a neat group of kids.

The second day the same thing happened. The kids were listening, learning, and enjoying the Bible lesson—when a noisy commotion broke out in the back of the room. Patti said nothing. She didn't need to. Tom was taking care of everything telling the kids to be quiet and listen to the lesson.

After class that day Patti asked Mrs. Deardorf, her assistant, to please teach the Bible lesson the next day. Mrs. Deardorf agreed and Patti continued praying. During recess on the third day Patti slipped to the back row and was busy reading and taking notes as the children filed into the room. Tom sat in the row in front of her, providentially one seat down where she could watch his every move as Mrs. Deardorf taught the lesson.

Mrs. Deardorf was good, and as the lesson became extremely interesting, and she had the complete attention of her audience, Tom studied the sharp pencil in his hand.

He glanced around the room, and then looked down at his pencil. Again he looked around, but every eye was on Mrs. Deardorf. No one but Patti saw that sharp pencil hit its target—the target was the little open space between where the back of the chair came down nearly to the back of the seat where Alfred* was sitting.

Alfred's body arose so quickly his knees hit the attached desktop making a resounding bang and his book and pencils went flying. He whirled around to face his tormentor and came face to face with Tom. The look on Alfred's face changed from anger to fear as he looked at Tom.

Soon Tom took over and had the whole room quiet again. Mrs. Deardorf looked at Patti with questioning eyes, but continued with her teaching, capturing the junior's attention again.

No one saw the very sharp pencil in Patti's trembling hand. No one watched as it found its mark in the little space between the back of the chair and the seat where Tom was sitting.

Patti hadn't known—for she hadn't seen—a person who could go straight up from a sitting position. *Oh, God did my anger make me act too quickly? Did it make me hit too hard?!*

This noise was even louder than the previous one! On his way down, Tom, with fire in his eyes, turned in mid air to face whoever was sitting behind him. All eyes were on Patti and Tom as she gave him her sweetest smile accompanied with a little wink—like "you and I have a secret." With one finger over her lips for everyone to be quiet, she used the other hand to motion for everyone to turn and look at the teacher just as she had seen Tom do. Strangely enough the room soon became quiet again. Alfred caught her eye, and the knowing look she gave him let him know that she had

---

*   Name has been changed

seen all that had happened a few minutes earlier.

The days flew by. No more disruptions. No more confusion. The juniors were absolutely great. One day after class, a junior boy whom she had just gotten acquainted with stopped by, and with tears in his eyes, explained that the next day he would be leaving to go back to live with his mother.

"I really tried to talk them into letting me stay." His words were broken. "But I have to go." Then he brightened. "Maybe I can find a Vacation Bible School like this in Klamath Falls."

Three big junior boys always sat on the front row intently listening to the lesson. They helped give Patti the courage she needed. One of the boys, whom she had become acquainted with for the first time in VBS class, stopped by her desk and asked many questions before leaving for home at the end of the day. It was a thrill when he decided to be baptized soon after the close of VBS.

She had just lived two weeks filled with excitement, challenge, and fulfillment. Why had it taken her so long to say "yes" to God?

Patti had learned something very important. God was someone she could trust. If He asked her to do something, and she did her best, He would be responsible for the results—in spite of the mistakes she seemed to make.

19

A New Home

Del was ready to build. Soon they would have their very own home. House plans lay on the table. The beautiful acre of land Patti's parents had given them for their new home lay nearly a quarter of a mile away. The property was smooth as a table top, but the thick alfalfa sod had to be dug out before the forms for the foundation were made.

As the home progressed and more lumber and building materials were delivered, Del became concerned that someone might come in to steal the material. He set up his own burglar alarm system. If someone intruded onto the place at night it would break a wire that would turn on the vacuum cleaner.

Several weeks later Patti awoke with a start. "Del, Del! The vacuum! The vacuum!"

Del was already out of bed and pulling on his clothes. Patti's dad had belonged to the Burns Detective Agency, so he was ready to go in no time. She heard the car pull out and race down the road. The clock on the dresser said two-thirty in the morning.

Time stood still until Patti heard the car coming up the road and drive down the driveway. Del quietly came into the house, worked with the vacuum cleaner a bit so it would automatically come on again, and tiptoed into the bedroom.

"Are you still awake? Whatever or whoever set off the alarm left before we arrived. We looked the place over carefully," he told her before he fell asleep.

Time hurried on as the months flew by. Decisions. Decisions. What kind of appliances should they get? What carpeting would be best? Which pieces of furniture should they buy? Finally, after years of dreaming and working, their new home was ready to move into.

The big freezer had been sitting outside, but now it was moved into the attached garage—already made into a family room.

That evening Del, Patti, Eddie and Judy relaxed and played on the new carpet watching the fire dancing in the fireplace. After prayers thanking God for His blessings and their new home, the children were tucked into bed in their own rooms and were soon fast asleep.

In the darkness of the night Patti suddenly was wide awake. Something strange was happening. She felt it. There was movement in the room. There was movement in her hair.

"Del, wake up!"

She lay frozen with surprise and fear. "Del, Del, there's something in my hair!"

"There's what?"

"Quick, Del, turn on the light. Quick."

Del switched on the light, and Patti saw a pack rat leap clear across the bed and hit the floor. The rat ran this way and that way around the room. Del grabbed a shoe, but was unable to touch the animal. Eddie heard the commotion and came running down the hall.

"Don't open the door," Del yelled to Eddie. "Please bring me a piece of two by four."

Eddie slipped through the door with the wood which was about two feet long, and the rat went up one side of Eddie and down the other. Now there were her two men after the rat. Patti stood in the middle of the bed trying to keep from screaming as she watched the rat actually jump and go halfway up the wall.

After a mighty battle, the rat was clobbered. Eddie went back to his bedroom, and Del fell asleep. Patti could not go back to sleep. There was another pack rat in the house! Although Del could not get the next pack rat out from where it had escaped, being an electrician, he soon had a device fixed that made the rat decide that under the dishwasher was not a comfortable place to be. When the second rat was gone, peace and quiet filled the house.

Days later Del called her. "I want to show you something." She tried to read his face as she followed him to the garage, and he told her to look in the back of the freezer. There was grass, straw, and sticks mixed in with the motor parts—a pack rat's nest! While Del and Patti had been building their new home, the big freezer had sat outside and a pair of pack rats had also been busy building their new home in the motor of the freezer.

"You thought we were just carrying in the freezer." Del's eyes twinkled. "But we brought you something extra."

20

More Challenges

Del and Patti continued working on their new home putting in landscaping and a large garden. But Patti felt miserable—very tired and sick. Her doctor said she was pregnant. Two months later the doctor decided there had been a mistake. She couldn't be pregnant, but something else must be extremely wrong. Betty, her cousin, came to help take care of her and the children. By now the fetus would have been about five months old, but she didn't even know she was pregnant because the little fetus had been dead for two or three months. Betty, a nurse, realized what was happening and let Patti know she had just lost a little baby. Then the doctor, when checking Patti's blood, found that she had a rare disease because of carrying a dead baby for so long.

Patti's sister-in-law took her to the Portland Sanitarium and stayed with her during many tests and treatments. *Was she going to die?* During the night in the hospital, Patti had a dream. She dreamed she saw a bright light. It was almost blinding. She heard a voice say, "You are going to die." In her dream she begged not to die because her two little children needed her. She cried and pleaded. "I just want to raise my children to serve the Lord. I must be here to teach them. I want Jesus to be their closest Friend. I want to meet them in heaven." The dream was vivid as she heard the voice say,

"You may live as long as your children need you."

"Blessed be the name of the Lord from this time forth and for evermore." Psalms 113:2.

Patti thanked God as she gradually gained strength and was able to take care of her family again. She did not forget that dream easily. With new determination she tried to teach her children to know and love the Lord. She would do her best with what time she had and leave the results with God.

Judy took pride in her pretty new bedroom. She arranged her dolls in a long row along the shelf under the big window with its frilly curtains that Patti had made. The curtains matched the pink bedspread Patti had created to fit Judy's new bed. This little five-year-old girl carefully smoothed out her bed every morning.

Eddie was pleased to have a room all his own in which to keep his assortment of treasures. His daddy had gotten him tools, and he spent many hours making a play house for Judy. That play house turned into a chicken house when he decided he wanted to raise some baby chicks. That was fine with Judy. She too enjoyed watching the fluffy little yellow chicks as they grew to be beautiful red hens laying eggs for the family meals.

Eddie was a very busy little boy, and the last thing he wanted to do was spend time cleaning his room. Patti felt making his bed before going out to play was essential—a rule Eddie didn't agree with!!

The third morning when she called him back—after he had slipped out of the house after breakfast without straightening his room—she knew he was deliberately disobeying. When she went outside and called him to come back into the house and finish his chores before going out to play, the look on Eddie's face and his body language told her volumes. He pulled the blue and white bedspread over the bunched up blankets and stalked out of the house.

He is only obeying that much because I am bigger than he is! With tears running down her face, Patti dashed to her bedroom. She dropped to her knees on the floor and prayed. "Oh, God, what have I done wrong? What should I do?"

She reached up to the stand beside her bed and while still on her knees opened the book *Child Guidance* by Ellen White. Right at the place where she had stopped reading the day before, she read, "Parents should teach their children by precept and example."

Patti caught her breath as she looked at her own unmade bed!! "Oh, dear God," she cried, "please forgive me. I scolded Eddie for having a bed that looks like mine!"

She usually slipped out of bed each morning and fixed Del's lunch while getting breakfast, and then after prayer, and he had gone to work, she cleaned the kitchen before straightening up her own bedroom.

The next morning after Del left for work, Patti whirled around and looked at the children. "I'll get my bed made before you do." Then she rushed to her bedroom. The game was on and there was no more problem with bed making. Of course, as Eddie got older and rules changed, the new one became, "Please, just keep your door closed so I don't have to see your bedroom!"

What would she do without that remarkable book *Child Guidance*? Years before the neighbor who had been taking care of the children for a couple of hours said, "The children slept the whole time I was here, so I just read this amazing book that was lying on the table by the couch." She held up the book *Child Guidance*. "I would give anything if I could have had a book like that when my children were little."

21

Help!!

Patti sat in the living room looking out the big window, but not seeing the large green lawn with shrubs lining the driveway. The array of colors flooding the flower beds begged for some notice, but her thoughts were far away.

Whittier Molding had sold the patent rights of the equipment Del helped design to a company located in Portland. That company had just called Del to see if he would move to Portland and work for them. Gordon Whittier, a friend of Del's, explained that if Del did not accept the good-paying job offered, the whole thing would probably fall on its face.

"If you really want to go to Portland," Patti's voice lacked enthusiasm, "of course I wouldn't try to persuade you to do anything else." Her mind flew to visions of all the things that had been rushing around both Del and her the past few months. After Whittier sold the equipment, Del had applied for a job teaching at Bend Community College. Instead, Lane Community College, near Eugene, had talked him into teaching math classes there. Patti had spent weeks going back and forth looking for a place to buy. She would go for a week at a time looking for places in the daytime and correcting test papers with Del in the evening—working in the sleeping room he was renting, that also came with kitchen privileges. She didn't worry about the children for they loved being with their grandparents. Weekends were fun when the family could all be together again.

They decided God must not want them to move to Eugene or else they could have found something that they liked and could afford. Del's heart remained in research. He turned down the offer to teach at the college the next school year, but had asked Patti to spend the last two weeks in Eugene with him, helping get all the test papers corrected and things closed up for the year.

She knew she should have been home preparing for Vacation Bible School. However, she had organized well with her wonderful helpers. Ione, a capable lady, would be her assistant. Ione had worked in the kindergarten department the year before. Patti could not ask for a better craft leader. Jeannette had also done crafts for the kindergarten class the previous year. Patti was definitely not prepared, but Del had needed her. She felt that she could delegate a lot, and with her mother's help, study each evening enough to keep ahead of her kindergarten children. Now everything had just tumbled around her feet and shattered like a broken piece of crystal.

"Oh, Patti, just think!" Jeannette looked at her with sparkling eyes. "I have been hired for this new job that I have wanted for so long. I will be starting to work full-time on Monday." Then she added, and some of the excitement had left her voice, "I hate to leave on such short notice, but the crafts this year are easy. I will come over and show you how to do them."

Easy! Beautiful things just fell off the ends of Jeannette's fingers. She was artistic and talented, and besides she liked doing things like that. Now she expected Patti to teach them to the children. They probably could learn faster on their own!

Patti sat on the couch and again looked out the window.

The bright blue sky held fluffy white clouds. The birds sang, and the mountains in the distance made a pretty picture, but she neither saw nor heard. She just sat there and then slowly turned toward her guests. How could she pull her mind back to the present and face the unbelievable?

Newel, Ione's husband, sat in a big easy chair and spoke with authority. "I've taken a logging job up in the mountains. I know you'll understand. You've been gone helping your husband. I really need Ione to come with me."

"I told him I wouldn't go unless we came over and talked to you first, and it was okay with you." Ione looked anxiously at Patti.

"I really need her." Newell sounded almost angry. "I know you'll understand. You have been able to go and help Del a lot. I want Ione to come with me."

Patti listened without energy, without strength, and without objections. *Oh, yes, of course I will not try to keep Ione from being with her husband. Oh, yes, of course I will understand.*

Her words trailed off brokenly. "Oh, yes, of…"

As Patti slowly closed the door behind Newell and Ione the room began to turn black. She tried to catch herself on the couch as she felt herself go down, down, down before oblivion struck.

22

The Answer

Patti opened her eyes. She was lying on the couch, with her head cradled on Del's lap. He patted her cheek. "I've been thinking, my dear. I don't want to move to Portland any more than you do. I don't have any obligation to work for that company even if Gordon is trying to make me think I do. Maybe they don't have the resources to make a success of that equipment. I didn't sell it to them. No." He looked into Patti's eyes. "We are not moving to Portland, and don't you worry about it anymore."

She sat up, wrapped her arms around her husband, and laid her head on his shoulder. "Oh, Darling, let Gordon move to Portland and work for that company if it is so important to him."

Patti watched Del walk back to the garage which had become a family room and now had been transformed into a research lab. He looked happy and prepared for anything. She knew that he would soon be immersed in momentous decisions in his quest to accomplish things that had never been done before.

Both children were interested in the Vacation Bible School kindergarten materials she brought in and spread out on the table. The telephone rang, and she struggled to answer it, as her mind tried to figure out how she could teach fifty or sixty little kindergarten children all by herself.

"Hello, Patti." Ione's voice came sweet and clear. "Newell and Glenn just left for the mountains. I told Newell I will go back with him in a couple weeks, but I just couldn't leave you like that. I will see you in the morning."

"Oh, Ione, you are a dear." Tears of relief flowed down Patti's cheeks.

With new energy she tackled her assignment for the next day and determined to be a part of the children's youthful zeal and enthusiasm for VBS. How many children would there be? No one knew. The year before they had prepared for forty, and over one hundred and twenty had come. However, this year Gordon had told Del that their large church was also having a VBS at the same time.

"We had to." He grinned at Del. "If we didn't, you would be getting all of our children."

Monday morning Patti's happiness overflowed as she looked into the excited eyes and smiling faces of the little children. She pleaded with God for His Holy Spirit to guide and touch the heart of each child.

Ione, having worked with crafts before, also took over that job. Three high school students came to help. They helped on the playground, helped with crafts, and helped by being friends with the children. Graduation night the children turned into angels and sang their little hearts out. Patti felt very proud of them. Vacation Bible School was worth everything they had put into it, and she hoped what the children had learned in those two short weeks would stay with them a lifetime.

Del's eyes shone with the pure fire of a great purpose. He glowed with inspiration and wondering interest as he made new discoveries on his invention. Patti wondered where he would get money to cover the extra living expenses in their new home, and make the car and house payments—and then she saw the check.

23

Working Again

"Del, did you know you were going to get a seven hundred dollar check from Lane Community College?"

"What? A seven hundred dollar check just came? Where did that come from?"

"Lane Community College."

"Why did they send it?"

Patti looked at Del in utter surprise. "Darling, how would I know why they sent it, but they did. Isn't it wonderful?"

Now they could pay their bills, and Del could still work the next few months full-time on his projects. They might be poor in worldly goods, but they were rich in dreams. The whole house seemed to spin into a research laboratory. Del was onto a great idea of how to check the moisture content in wood electronically. There were days and nights when the bathtub soaked lumber. Other days and nights their new built-in oven dried lumber.

The kitchen table turned into a desk as Patti typed letters and helped order parts. Little money was spent on parts, for most of them came from old radios and television sets. The radios and television sets hung onto their parts with perseverance while Patti tried to dissect them. She felt she needed at least one or two more hands to do the job properly. Yes, she knew Del did it with precision and efficiency, but school had never prepared her for taking radios and televisions apart. She would leave the research project for Del and go find another job.

Patti got a job in Redmond. She was able to visit with the children in the morning while taking them to school on her way to work. In the afternoon another mother took them to their grandparent's place to stay until she got home from the office, or they could come home if Del was there.

Making out reports on how many tons of potatoes were being shipped out of the county seemed important to the company Patti worked for. The important part to her was that it paid good money. Even counting potatoes gave her more of a feeling of accomplishment than breaking valuable little radio parts while trying to amputate them for Del to use later.

One busy afternoon, Irene the office manager, appeared concerned. "Patti, you look awful. Why don't you go home and rest?" Patti's head throbbed, and she felt hot and tired, but she wanted to finish a report on time.

"I will." She studied the papers on her desk. "First I want to finish this report."

Much later, the columns finally balanced, and Patti walked out the door of the building. She drove home, parked the car, and walked into the house. As she stepped into the kitchen, a disarray of clutter faced her. Seven-year-old Judy, wearing one of Patti's aprons, continued stirring something in a big bowl. Nine-year-old Eddie had a cookbook in his hand reading a recipe to Judy.

When the children turned to greet her, Eddie looked frustrated, and she saw tears in Judy's eyes. They had planned a lovely dinner to surprise her, but nothing had turned out like the pictures in the book. Patti's heart burst with love and compassion at the sight of these dear, willing "helpers."

The project of the moment was a cake they were trying to make from scratch. Patti tasted the cake batter. She did not know what it contained, but determined the cake would be a success. With a little of this and a little more of that, the cake (now two cakes) turned out fine. Then with help from their mother, Eddie and Judy had the rest of the meal ready to serve.

The glow in Patti's heart soothed her body. The children had been working for hours to make this a special occasion. When she told them the food tasted wonderful, she meant every word of it.

Patti struggled through the evening not letting the children know how badly she felt. Nothing was going to spoil the enjoyment of this time she had with her precious children, who had worked so hard to surprise her.

Finally the kitchen was clean, the evening was over, and Patti crawled into bed. Del would take the children to school the next day. The office did not need her. *Should I mention to the children that it might be better to wait until I am home to do the complicated cooking jobs? No, I will not disappoint them in that way—never, never, never.*

24

On the Road

Del walked into the living room waving a check. He had just returned from a business trip.

"I sold my first piece of equipment!" he beamed.

"For one thousand six hundred dollars?" Patti stared at the check.

"Of course. It has already saved the company thousands of dollars."

The manager of a lumber mill had given Del permission to come to his plant, and do some experiments with the new equipment Del recently had finished designing. Del had installed the moisture detector sensors in an area just below the lumber which was on its way to a location to be sorted or run through a planer. The lumber traveled over the sensors on conveyer chains.

The equipment Del designed, automatically measured the moisture in each piece of lumber without touching it. If any piece of lumber had more moisture in it than the amount that was set on a control panel, that piece of lumber would be marked with a little squirt of colored liquid. The marked piece of lumber could then be pulled out and dried. Del also had a way of having the boards automatically separated from the rest of the lumber, so they could be sent back to the dry kiln to be dried, if that was what the mill personnel wanted to do.

After a few months, the manager at the mill was so impressed by what was being accomplished with this equipment, he did not want to be without it. He had the owners purchase the system.

This man had no idea the equipment had been made from old radio and television parts. Neither did he have any idea a few months later, when Del came to make some repairs, that the old system was replaced with a new moisture detection system—made with all new parts.

Del built a shop behind the house where he could cut and weld the iron. He also built shelves for the assembly work. With the assembling of instruments in the new building, the garage became an office with desks and filing cabinets.

The children helped by sorting parts, putting them into little drawers, and stuffing and stamping envelopes. Patti had quit her job, and now typed instruction books on how to install the equipment. She also typed manuals on how to run the equipment. Helping to assemble the instruments was not something that Patti liked to do, and she finally told Del that she hated putting all those tiny parts together. "Why didn't you tell me, Honey?" He then hired a part-time assembler.

It was necessary to show the equipment to potential buyers, so Del designed and built a box that covered most of the floor of their new van. It became a bed for the night and a container for their sleeping bags and personal belongings during the day. When he set up the equipment for display on top of the box, no one knew it was used to sleep in at night— usually by one person while the other drove. In that way they were able to visit all of the lumber mills in the Northwest.

"Oh, look." Del was driving over the mountains in Montana one snowy night. "There was the most beautiful elk in front of me, and I wanted you to see it."

The elk had disappeared, but the moon and stars covered

the newly fallen snow with silver. Patti crawled from her bed and slid into the seat beside Del to enjoy the beauty with him. Together they watched the tumbling water cutting through the bank of white as it cascaded down the mountain. They both marveled at the loveliness of God's creation.

Early one November morning, on another business trip, while crossing the Rocky Mountains in British Columbia—the first snow of the season welcomed them. This time they were driving a car. Del had planned to get a new set of snow tires before leaving for this northern part of the country. However, the time pressure of the trip had hampered that. The tires definitely needed replacing, and they refused to hang on to the slippery pavement. Patti could feel the car sliding and turning this way and that.

"Oh, no! Dear Lord, please help us!"

The car was out of control!!

It looked like the trees were moving swiftly towards them—and then she felt the car plunge toward the canyon below.

25

The Good Samaritan

Off the road and down the bank the car flew—right into a fir tree big enough to stop the fall, but small enough to bend under the impact of the vehicle. Neither Del nor Patti were injured, and the car was still drivable although it looked like it had been in a fight. After the wrecker had pulled them out, and they limped down the road in a battered car, Del decided they did have time to stop and get a new set of snow tires!

"The angel of the Lord encampeth round about them that fear Him, and delivereth them." Psalm 34:7. Del and Patti had a little praise service thanking God for His protection.

One special Sabbath morning Patti sat on the edge of her seat in the little white church—where she and Del had first become husband and wife—listening to a dynamic speaker. Luke 10:25-37 came alive and burnt its self into her conscience. The pastor brought his message across with enthusiasm. "Yes, it was dangerous for the Good Samaritan to stop and help another human in trouble, and yes, sometimes it is hard to help, but what does Jesus expect us to be doing now?"

With a determination, lacking good, well-balanced judgment, Patti decided that the next time she saw anyone in need, she would stop and help.

Del decided to take a business trip to Canada. Patti knew

that they would be traveling through some of the most beautiful country in the world, and determined that she would take the children to see the breath-taking mountains of British Columbia.

She talked with the children's teacher and got the assignments for their studies. Very seldom did the family have a chance to be traveling together, and she enjoyed every minute of it. The children insisted that they would be enjoying it more if they did not have to do their studies before being allowed to play each day.

After a few days of travel, study, and fun together, the whole family headed for home. Del, as usual, wanted to be home putting more moisture detectors together and filling the orders that he had received.

"Let's drive late tonight." He started the car and headed for Oregon. Hour after hour he drove. Patti made a bed on the floor for Eddie. Judy was already sleeping in the back seat of the car. The children looked comfortable. Del seemed wide awake and anxious to keep going, so she leaned her head on the back of the seat and slept.

"Patti, can you drive now? I am so tired. I have to get some sleep."

She glanced at her watch. It said three in the morning. "Are you planning to drive all the way home?"

"Why not?" He looked at her and smiled. "I can drive after a few hours, but I need to stretch out. Do you think the children could sleep in the front seat for a little while?"

Del spread himself across the back seat, and the children slept in the front beside Patti. She could see the moon peaking through the clouds as she drove in the early morning hours. With everyone sleeping, she spent her time talking with God. *"I do want to help those in need,"* she told Him. As she watched the dawn of a new day begin to flood the

Eastern sky, Patti began to see the trees on the mountains around. On the left side of the road she saw a high bank. A river ran along on the right side. Coming around a corner she noticed a car to her right. She could make out the forms of three people. It appeared to her that they were begging for assistance.

"Del, wake up! Somebody needs help. Del! Del!"

Patti put on the brakes and rolled to a stop a little distance behind the other car.

"Del, wake up. I need you!"

By now both of the children were wide awake.

"Daddy, Daddy, wake up."

"Daddy, wake up!" Eddie was leaning over the back of the seat almost shouting in Del's ear.

The people began walking towards the car. They stopped, forming a little circle, conversing among themselves for a few moments, while Patti continued to try to awaken Del.

"Del, Del! What shall I do?"

Next Patti watched the little circle break up. A young man walked to the left of the car. A young man with a woman approached the right side.

"Del, Del, please just wake up!" *Oh, God what shall I do? Del won't wake up! Please, God, tell me what to do*!

At that moment an urge so strong she had never felt anything like it before hit Patti. It was, *"GET OUT OF HERE AS FAST AS YOU CAN."*

26

Growing, Growing, Growing

Three young people were slowly walking towards the car and were only a foot or two away. Patti hit the gas pedal. The car shot ahead. No one said a word for a mile or two while Patti continued driving down the road.

"Mother, why did you do that?" Eddie's eyes were big with wonder. "You acted like you were going to help those people—and then took off spinning gravel like crazy when they were nearly to the car."

"I didn't know what to do. Daddy wouldn't wake up, and I couldn't ask him what to do. I didn't know what Daddy wanted me to do."

Patti and the children talked a few more minutes while she wondered what could be wrong with Del. *How could he still be sleeping? Something definitely must be the matter. Had he driven too long?* Then she saw Del sit up and look around.

"Daddy, why didn't you wake up? We called and called."

"I don't know what you are talking about." Del had a surprised, questioning look. "I didn't hear anyone calling me."

"We called and called, and you wouldn't answer." The children were both talking now. "Why didn't you wake up?"

Something out of the ordinary had kept Del asleep, for

he was not a heavy sleeper. He always woke up easily. Could it have been the angels who had kept him from being awakened? They never knew, but thanked God for His guidance and protection from an experience that could have ended in tragedy.

In the spring of 1969 Patti and Del came bursting into the house from a long trip, happy to be home again. "Where are the children?" Patti looked around the room. It already was getting late.

"They are out with Grandpa selling Pathfinder candy." Her mother finished putting the things away she had in her hands. "I believe tonight is the last night they will be going out selling. They are almost finished, and they are so excited. Those two have sold more candy than anyone else."

Patti heard the slamming of car doors, and two children, with glowing faces, rushed in with a whirl seeing who could get there the fastest. Grandpa came in behind them. He looked as if he had been having a good time too.

"We sold all the candy," they bubbled. "We didn't even save any to sell to you."

Del and Patti laughed and hugged them both. "What are you raising money for?"

"We are going to the Redwoods in California, and we're going to camp at the Rogue River Park on the way. Oh, Daddy and Mother, you are supposed to come too."

That sounded exciting to Patti. She always tried to be involved in whatever the children were doing when she was home. The children were growing up so fast. Eddie had insisted that he now was "Ed," not "Eddie."

"We have sold more candy and raised more money than anyone else."

Patti let the children know how proud they were of them. Of course she knew something they did not realize. Her parents had lived in this home since she was a child; and although they were busy hard-working people, they never were too busy to help a person in need or stop a minute to visit. She knew the neighbors for miles around would buy the candy whether they wanted it or not.

When the day for the camping trip arrived, she helped the children load all of their camping gear into the van. She and Berta, another mother, would drive the loaded van. When the cars were filled with Pathfinders, the little caravan headed for the long anticipated adventure—the Redwoods of California.

Patti felt disappointed, but not surprised, that she had not been able to talk Del into going camping with them. *Why did this business have to rule them with such an iron hand?*

When Judy gave her piano recital, the business dictated that Del be somewhere else. *How many little eleven-year-old girls gave a recital—from memory?* Ed and a friend, Scott, also played some songs to give Judy a break. People packed into the school building; but Judy's daddy was not there. Of course he had heard the songs before, and the house had echoed with scales, arpeggios, melody, harmony, and disharmony (at times) in the early morning and evenings.

Patti wished Del would not be so intense in his work. To make her happy, he did say he would visit some businesses along the way, and then spend one night in California with the group of Pathfinders.

He drove in late the second evening of the camping trip and was there to enjoy the last song around the campfire, listen to the children tell of camping by the Rogue River, and watched while they pointed out where they had seen a herd of elk.

Then the time came for everyone to be in their tents for the night, so the children scampered off to their assigned places, while Del and Patti set up camping in the van. After they had spread out the sleeping bags and arranged things for the night, Del put his arms around Patti and looked into her face as they stood under the stars by the camper. "Listen, Honey, I bought a five acre place in Rogue River. You will love it. It is very nice."

Patti was stunned. "You bought us a new place to live in Rogue River, when you came through today—just like that!?"

27

Expansion

Del and Patti had been looking for a place where they could move, that was located close to a ten or twelve-grade Christian Academy. Ed would be finishing eighth grade soon, and they would like to have the children home for a few more years before going away to a boarding school. They also wanted their new home to be in a better location that would be more conducive for the growing business.

"You will really like this place." Del held Patti in his arms while she tried to come out of shock. "I couldn't let it slip out of our hands. The people were very anxious to sell right away. They are an exceptionally nice older couple. You must meet them soon. Their name is Wein, and they own the Wein Alaska Airlines."

"I have lived in more luxurious places." Mrs. Wein walked around the residence, showing Patti her new country home. "But I have never lived in a home that I enjoyed more. It is only three years old."

Del and Patti had been praying that God would direct them where they should move, and He had provided this lovely home for them in beautiful southern Oregon. Del hired carpenters to build a big shop, so production could keep going when they moved.

Now Patti was getting a nice, large office. Del had an office of his own, room for the assemblers, a research lab, and a back room used for cutting and welding.

Patti stopped traveling with Del and stayed home with the children. Ed's music lessons changed from piano to guitar, and Judy added accordion and flute. Patti was on the road so much taking the children to appointments, she wondered why they even needed a house.

Ed learned to do everything in the business; cutting and welding the machinery, assembling the instruments, and anything else that needed to be done. When Ed was sixteen years old, he went here and there and everywhere picking up needed things for the business. With the confidence of a newly licensed driver, it was one of his favorite jobs.

Another desk had been moved into the main office. Roberta, the new secretary, was efficient and fun. When the children went away to boarding academy, Patti started traveling with Del again when it was convenient.

Patti felt almost dizzy with concern. "I think we should cancel this trip." They had locked the house, and settled in the car headed for the airport in Medford, Oregon.

"Why?" Del started the engine. "Surely the weather isn't that bad."

"Please, Darling, let us stay in Atlanta and take care of business there before flying to Buffalo, New York," Patti begged.

"We can decide that later." He was in a hurry to get to the airport in time.

"We can't. You have to decide where you want our luggage sent."

Del frowned. "Honey, why are you always afraid? I know how to drive in snow. If people are getting through, we can too. We need to make this sale. The fellow wanted me to come right away."

Oh, why was she going on this trip? She hated traveling on bad roads; and now they were headed straight for a blizzard. She had not planned to come, but during her morning devotions a few days before, she had felt impressed to come with Del.

Patti closed her eyes. *Dear God, I didn't want to come on this trip, but felt You wanted me to. I know You will be in charge. Right now I am asking for peace. Please, Lord, give me peace of mind.*

She could see the morning sky flushed with spreading light. Del flipped the switch on the radio. The first words they heard were, "All travel in the Buffalo, New York, and surrounding area, is illegal other than emergency vehicles. Anyone else trying to travel in these areas will be fined."

28

Protection

Del turned off the radio and said, "Let's send the luggage to Atlanta." He smiled at Patti and squeezed her hand. She closed her eyes. *Thank You, God. Thank You for the reminder that You can do anything.* She still did not know the reason for her going on this trip, but as the peace of God filled her heart, she knew she was doing the right thing.

There was snow on the ground as the big plane landed at the Atlanta Airport. The icy wind slashed across her face when they stepped outside of the building. Everyone was talking about the cold spell that had hit the South.

As Patti walked to the rental car she saw waiting for them, she shivered in spite of her winter clothing and heavy coat. Del stopped and looked at the car while the cold bit into Patti.

"A Lincoln?" questioned Del. "I didn't order a Lincoln."

"Isn't it okay? Can't we take it?" shivered Patti.

"We only need a mid-sized car."

"Let's get in. I would like to take it."

"No. We can't afford a Lincoln."

"Maybe there was a mistake. Look at the papers."

"It says a Lincoln." Del studied the papers in his hand. "I'd better go back and get this straightened out."

"Is it costing you more than you planned?" Patti's teeth were chattering, while they stood outside in the biting wind and snow.

"Well—no—."

"Then let's take the Lincoln." Patti opened the door. "I think I'll like it."

That Lincoln, not like some of the other cars they had rented, stayed warm and comfortable. *Thank You, Lord.*

By the time they had gotten settled for the evening in Mobile, Alabama, a few days later, Del felt miserable. "I'll just go to bed early, but I'll be fine in the morning."

The next morning he looked wretched. "I am not feeling a bit well. I think you should get me something at the drug store."

He had been hot and restless during the night. Hastily finding a drug store, she bought some things from the Pharmacy along with a thermometer. Del's temperature exceeded 103 degrees.

"Darling, we've got to get home." Patti sobbed in desperation.

"No." Del looked up from the bed where he was lying. "There are hospitals here if we need one. Go call Dr. Kattenhorn."

The druggist talked to Dr. Kattenhorn, and then gave Patti some medicine. The medication helped, and Del slept. His temperature had come down to 102 degrees.

The next morning after he awoke from a fairly good night's sleep, Del looked at the clock. "Let's head toward Tallahassee, Florida."

"Oh, no! You are too sick." Patti felt alarm.

"I can sleep as well in the car as here. You go ahead and load it. Then after you get it warmed up, I'll get in and can rest all the way."

It was a bitterly cold Sunday morning. Patti did not see anyone around. All sensible people were probably shut away inside their warm motel rooms. She drove the Lincoln as close to the door of their room as she could, and started carrying one load after another out of the motel, and packed the bags into the trunk of the car. That is when she noticed a man halfway across the parking lot watching her every move. About ten minutes later while Patti searched to find a spot for the last piece of equipment, she heard hurried footsteps and looked up to see the man coming towards her. She closed the trunk of the car as swiftly and nonchalantly as she could. Quickly she went into the motel room locking the door behind her. Peeking through the curtains she saw the man turn and go up the stairs.

Patti tried to tell Del about the man, but what was there to tell? Besides, her husband appeared too sick to even listen to her worries. Next, she saw the man go to his car, drive it over to their room, and park it about as close behind the Lincoln as he could. Patti watched through the curtains as the man then walked from the parking lot, crossed the boulevard, and headed towards a nearby store. Del seemed eager to get going, but in no way more enthusiastic about it than Patti, at this moment. Hastily she got him into the car, but there seemed to be no possibility of getting the car out of the spot it was in. The other car, directly behind, had blocked the way. Back and forth, back and forth she went, praying all the time. Finally, and she knew it had to be a miracle—the Lincoln was free and heading for the street.

As she looked to the right before going onto the isolated street, she saw the man running down the sidewalk. He rushed to his car, jumped into it, and pulled up right behind her. Patti drove down the lonely street about ten miles an hour. The other car stayed behind so close it was almost touching her, following her, block after block after block. *Now what do I do?* "*Oh, God,* what shall I do?"

29

So Far

"Del, pull your car seat up to a sitting position and sit up high, so the man in the car behind will know I am not alone."

Del was so miserable he hardly knew what to do, but after a few questions and a few groans, did as she requested. A moment later, with the roar of a motor and tires squealing, the car veered around them and shot down the street.

"What was that?" Del peered out the window.

"The man I've been trying to tell you about."

"You mean that's the man in the parking lot?" Del appeared wide awake and all ears now. "Why didn't we do something about it?"

Patti just smiled. "We're fine now. Put your seat back and get some rest."

He did not put his seat back, but continued to watch the surroundings. "That guy must be crazy. I've never seen anyone drive like that before in my life."

After a time Del relaxed and slept like a baby while the miles sped behind them. She enjoyed driving this beautiful new car.

Oh, no, how could this be? She felt her heart speed up as her car slowed down, and her hands began to sweat. Del awoke as she pulled to the side of the road. Flashing red lights in the rearview mirror told Patti that the new Lincoln must have been really moving.

The officer spoke kindly as Patti told him of her sick husband, but explained in detail the hazards of speeding. Then looking over at Del said, "You'd better get him to the hospital right away. I'll write this ticket quickly so you can hurry." He told her the direction to the hospital at the next town and turned to go, then coming back he said, "Now don't go over the speed limit on your way."

She assured him that she wouldn't. She didn't either. That bright blue car followed her all the way to the next town. She turned off at the exit to the hospital and found the street where it was located. Then the Police car turned and went another direction.

Patti drove around the block and sat there awhile, resting. She saw a fast food restaurant and stopped to get something for Del and herself, but both felt too miserable to eat. She rested a few more minutes and then headed for the freeway again. The miles flew by, but not very fast. She did not like getting speeding tickets, and anyway, she felt so very tired.

At six that evening, she stopped at a little town. "We're staying here for the night," she told Del.

"Oh, Honey, we can't. We still have two more hours to go."

"I can't help it. I'm so tired I can't drive another mile."

"Well, why didn't you tell me? You just stretch out here and sleep. I'm feeling much better now."

Two hours later Patti awoke as Del stopped at a motel. She took her temperature. *Over 102 degrees! So that is why I feel so miserable. I'm glad Del is feeling better—or is he?*

Del, sitting at a small table, called the salesman at home. He asked him to go see some of the mills that Del had planned to see, but Patti could tell by the conversation that Forry, the salesman, was also sick.

"Really?" she heard Del say, "Then if you feel like that, they will have to wait. I just took my temperature this evening, and it is nearly 103 degrees, too."

Patti felt her head swimming. *Why do we have to be sick so far from home? I want to go home. Oh, how I want to go home. No use mentioning it to Del. "Why go home?" he would say.*

Yes, why go home? There are probably plenty of Funeral Homes in this town too, in case we need one.

30

Air Trouble

Patti lay in the motel room between the clean white sheets, but her body felt hot and her head ached.

What would Del have done being so sick if she had not come? And the car—they had never gotten a Lincoln before—but, they had never needed one before. God arranged things for their comfort before they even knew they needed it.

The text in Isaiah 65:24 flashed through Patti's mind. *"Before they call I will answer. While they are yet speaking I will hear."* The Lincoln had made the long trip much easier on both of them. She was cradled in the arms of a wonderful peace as she drifted into a comfortable sleep—that lasted the entire night.

Some of Del's medication and a good all day's rest in the motel that day, while he went to appointments to meet with the mill personnel, helped Patti begin to feel she would probably live.

The next day she was ready to go. She could rest as well in the car as in the motel—well not quite. Del did the driving as they headed for the airport to catch their flight to Boston.

On board the plane Patti laid her head back on the seat, hoping to get a little rest, as the great machine soared through the inky blackness. The weather had not been good. She did not expect it to be any better when they arrived at their destination, but the big storms were past and the roads plowed. She watched the attendants giving out the soft drinks and sugar peanuts.

Usually Patti took some, but not tonight. This was Tuesday. She had heard James Dobson tell how he and Shirley fasted and prayed all day for their children on Tuesdays. He told how God answers prayer. He had talked about the importance of God's protection and guidance for the young people who face many temptations. He enumerated the blessings that had come to his family, and especially his children, because of their Special Tuesdays.

His children are not better than mine. My children need prayer as much as his. They will not be denied that privilege.

Starting the next Tuesday, Patti's children had prayers going up to heaven for them all day. When the hunger pangs hit, she remembered what that day was all about and pleaded with God for His guidance in their lives.

"All attendants take your seats **now**," a voice came over the loud speaker. "We will be coming into some rough air."

Patti watched as one attendant rushed to a seat across the aisle and quickly fastened his seat belt. Another attendant tried to help the people in the front of the plane, swiftly removing some of their drinks, but it was too late. The plane felt like it was out of control. The stewardess dropped to the floor and came down the aisle on her stomach holding onto the legs of the seats for safety. She crawled into the seat beside the other flight attendant, and he hurriedly fastened her seat belt.

Patti hung on as the plane bounced and shuddered from the sudden drops. The passengers sat silent or spoke in hushed tones. She sat there pleading for God's protection. *Was this the way the boat felt out on the Sea of Galilee when the disciples were so afraid?* She tried to picture Jesus right beside her on that bouncing plane. She watched the lightning as it flashed outside her window. She thought about their guardian angels riding along with them. Del knew how she felt, and he held her tight. She had no idea how he was feeling. He always seemed so brave, confident, kind, and calm. She glanced across the aisle over at the attendants and saw perspiration running down the fellow's face.

"Aren't you afraid the man will lose his arm?"

Patti looked at the person speaking. The voice was attached to the flight attendant looking straight at her.

"What do you mean?" Patti's eyes were big with wonder.

"You are hanging on so tightly, you are shutting off all the blood."

Del gave her a little squeeze. The airplane was traveling through the air a bit smoother now. Time passed slowly before the voice on the loud speaker told the attendants they could now pick up the glasses. It did not come before the attendant had filled Del in on other horrifying experiences he had gone through in storms. *Why did Del keep asking him questions?* Patti tried to close her ears.

The voice on the loud speaker said, "We have crossed through the path of a thunder storm and will be landing soon."

Patti floated down the aisle; her feet were hardly touching as she started to disembark.

"You must be coming home," a stewardess commented. "Your face is radiant. Do you live in Boston?"

"No, I don't live in Boston." Patti giggled. "But I'm about to touch mother earth."

Snow was piled high on each side of the freeway. The snowplows were running and there was salt on the surface of the thoroughfare.

"They sure ruin the cars back here, with all of this salt."

Del was complaining, but Patti was delighted not to be slipping and sliding around.

"Why are you worried about this rental car?" Patti couldn't help but giggle. "I am sure it has seen a lot of salt before we ever got here."

They drove miles on the snowy roads to get to Del's appointments, but it was better than Patti had been expecting. Although it was stormy and cold, the snowplows and other road equipment were doing a great job. *Why don't they use salt on the icy roads back home in Oregon?*

Friday came and Del was ready to head home, but first they were to spend a quiet weekend resting and recuperating.

Wearing their long johns and other heavy winter clothes, they drove through the icy wind and snow to the airport. It would be warm at the end of their destination, but Patti had no desire to freeze if their little rental car stalled while pushing its way through the snow. From there they flew directly to the Caribbean Islands.

The flight was uneventful and beautiful. It was exciting seeing the green landscape, the white sand, and palm trees. What a wonderful change. Patti loved every minute of it. But as they walked from the terminal to their transportation, it felt like they had just entered an oven turned up ready to broil or roast them. Most everyone was in shorts and tee-shirts. Not Del and Patti—they were wearing heavy winter coats and boots. What else could they do? Their arms were full just carrying the luggage.

When they got to their older hotel, it didn't take them long to change into swim suits and run down to the beautiful white beach before plunging into the water.

Time goes too fast in a place like this, and before they knew it, Sunday had arrived. It was time to pack the suitcases again and head for the airport.

The problem . . . everyone else had the same idea. People were lined up at the elevator here on sixth floor. The elevator was coming up. They could see the numbers change 2—3—4—and then 1 again. The elevator started back up again 2—5—and then 3—4—1. "That elevator goes where it is pushed the last time." Back and forth it went. Time was wasting. Would they make it to the airport in time?

31

An Unforgettable Bus Ride

Del and Patti were on the sixth floor of the hotel anxious to check out and get to the airport, but the old elevator in the building was having a problem. Whenever anyone pushed the button it would forget what it was supposed to do and head in the direction of the last push. Back and forth—up and down it went. No one could go anyplace. Too many people were waiting to get on that elevator and pushing buttons.

"We'll fix that." Del pushed the elevator button again and again. 1—push 2—push 3—push. Del kept pushing the button. 4—push 5—push 6—push. The elevator stopped and the door opened. Everyone shoved their way in and down it started 5—4—6—7—. Oh, no. Del started pushing the buttons again, and finally they were on first floor and rushing to check out of the hotel. Next it was out the door to the transportation car and on to the airport.

Finally on the big plane, Patti felt extremely happy. She fastened her seat belt and then watched the land disappear behind them as they were lifted into the cloudless sky. They had made it in time.

"We are turning back." Del was watching out the window.

"Please, Honey, don't tease me now. I want to get home

so badly."

"I am not teasing."

Sitting behind a couple of attendants and listening to the quiet communication, they became aware that the plane was dumping thousands of gallons of gasoline into the ocean in an effort to get back to the island.

When the pilot brought the plane down in a perfect landing, many people began complaining, for they did not know what Del and Patti knew. She did not complain and kept busy thanking God for His protection and bringing them back to a safe landing.

They sat in the grounded jet for an hour. No one could leave. Every fifteen minutes or so a voice would tell them there would be a few more minutes to wait. Then after the hour wait, everyone had to leave the aircraft.

Del tried to glean information, but none was forthcoming. When he asked an attendant why they dumped the gasoline, she looked surprised.

"To help us have a safe landing." She spoke very quietly and acted as if she and Del had a secret.

After three more hours, they were ordered back on the SAME airplane. What needed fixing? What had they done? Even Del could not get that information.

They changed aircrafts in Atlanta. "I feel safer now." Patti squeezed Del's hand. "We are almost home!"

The excursion Del and Patti took to Puerto Rico some time later was for a rest—a much needed rest in a beautiful land where palm trees lined the beaches and the golden sun sank into the ocean as they strolled along the water's edge. Patti and Del did not patronize the resorts or spend time in the elegant neighborhoods. Instead they rode the busses and mingled with the needy.

One evening in the city of San Juan, they had taken bus

ride after bus ride. *Now where was their hotel?* Del quietly asked the man across the aisle if he knew the location of the Silver Sand Hotel. The man then said something in Spanish to someone else who said something to someone else in Spanish. Soon people began telling them where to go. It seemed that half of the people on the bus were in on the discussion arguing over where Del and Patti should get off the bus. One person after another would try to get Del to get off the bus with them, before they climbed down the stairs and were gone.

Patti's SOS's were ascending to God in rapid succession while she watched a couple of fellows almost come to blows, trying to outtalk each other in convincing Del where he should get off the bus.

A lady sitting in front of them moved to an empty seat that was right behind the bus driver. Patti saw the two people talking back and forth in a rather animated conversation. Then the lady came back to where she had been sitting and sat down. Carefully she slipped Patti a piece of paper. On it were written the words, "DON'T GET OFF. STAY WHERE YOU ARE."

32

A Stranger's Help

Del and Patti sat on the bus wondering what would happen next. One man stood at the doorway waiting to depart, he motioned for them to come. "I will show you where to go." He spoke in broken English.

Patti heard the bus driver say something to the man in Spanish. The man seemed startled for a moment. Then he studied the driver through wicked eyes and gave him a dreadfully nasty look. A moment later, the evil-looking man turned and went out the door and down the steps of the bus.

The lights of the city were ablaze. Everyone but Patti and Del seemed to know the bus was not following its regular route. The people on the bus started complaining and shouting in Spanish. The bus driver silenced them, but Del and Patti had no idea what he said. The bus hurried down the road. No one was getting off, but sat, stony faced, where they were.

After a few more miles and a few more turns, Del grabbed Patti's trembling arm. "Look! There is our hotel!"

The bus came to a stop close to the big front doors of the building. The driver motioned for them to get off, and they quickly departed thanking the driver for his kindness. The bus continued to wait until they were safely inside the hotel. Then it slowly turned around and went back in the direction from where it had come.

"Praise ye the Lord. I will praise the Lord with my whole heart . . ." Psalm 111:1. *Thank You. Thank You, God!!* They hurried up the stairs to their room to have a little praise service thanking God for His protection.

On another adventure Patti sat in the Atlanta Airport looking out the window at the many airplanes coming and going. As they had approached the landing that morning, she watched another plane skimming the earth. It looked as if the other plane would hit them. Even Del seemed a little startled. The attendant was watching too, but said, "Don't worry. Everything is under control."

Everything **did** seem to be under control for the many planes as they lined up behind each other, waiting to take to the clear blue sky.

What about Del and me? Are our lives under control? Do we know what we are doing on this trip? "Dear, God," Patti pleaded, *"please be in control of our lives. Please take care of us. Thank You, Lord. Amen."*

Del and Patti traveled visiting most of the lumber mills all over the United States. Many times they would fly Eastern Airlines, taking their unlimited flights. The schedule must be made thirty days in advance. They could go anywhere, with as many flights as they wanted, for three whole weeks—anywhere, that is, where Eastern Airlines flew.

It was not unusual for Del to make an appointment with a mill, maybe in Texas, for one day; then fly to another mill in someplace like Minnesota the next day. He would meet with someone in Arkansas another day, then fly to Virginia or some other far-away place that evening to meet someone there before catching the plane the next afternoon. It could be Alabama, or Mississippi, or maybe Florida. This would be the schedule for three whole weeks!

Many times they had to catch a plane going to Atlanta, change planes, and head back to a territory close to where they had been before. The day they left New York to go to Washington, DC, Del tried to see if he could get another flight. It seemed like such a waste of time to have to go through Atlanta! However, they were not complaining. The tickets were only seven hundred dollars each for the whole three weeks of travel, and the food was abundant with snacks all the way.

The difficult schedule of catching a plane every other day or so—sometimes every day—was compensated for by the wonderful weekends when they would fly to some exotic spot to spend a relaxing day or two.

This day they were waiting for the plane to leave for Mexico City. The room filled with excited people. Many were speaking Spanish.

"Where are you staying in the city?" a man sitting beside Del asked.

"We haven't made arrangements yet," he answered.

"Do you speak Spanish?" someone wanted to know.

"No."

"It is best if you exchange your money for the currency you will need before you go," someone else said.

The time passed slowly. As more and more people kept giving them advice, even Del became concerned that they had not prepared properly for this trip.

"I am going down to exchange some money." He stood and started to walk away.

"Not on your life! The plane is about to leave. What would I do if it started loading and you weren't here?" Patti began to feel the stress consuming her.

A lady had been sitting close by quietly listening. She looked at Patti and said, "I think you need someone to take care of you."

117

33

An Awesome God

The huge plane began loading, and Patti felt somewhat content with Del by her side. They could worry about getting the right money later.

Coming down the stairs into the lobby at the airport in Mexico City, they saw a sea of heads. The place was so crowded she wondered how they could even walk through. *How would they ever find their baggage? Of course they would never see that lady again. She probably was just making conversation and being friendly.*

"You stand in this line." Del showed Patti where to stay. "Get our money exchanged while I get our baggage. Don't leave. Wait right here. I could never find you again if you go any other place."

Patti got the money exchanged. Then she waited. *Would Del ever come? How could he even find their things in such a crowd?* It seemed like hours before she saw him heading her way in the middle of a mass of people. She had a hard time believing her eyes. The lady and her husband who had talked to Patti in Atlanta looked like guardian angels walking beside Del with their luggage on a big cart along with Del's belongings.

"Since we don't have any plans," Del spoke quietly, "we might as well get a room at the same hotel as these people.

She speaks Spanish and will get a taxi. It costs less if we go together."

Patti tingled with excitement. That lady really did mean that Del and she needed someone to take care of them. She had appointed herself as their helper. Again Patti thanked her Heavenly Father for His constant care.

The taxicab driver loaded the trunk full of bags. He placed some of them on the back seat; Del and Patti slid in beside them. Their new friend, Cynthia, and her husband, Doug, sat in the front where Cynthia could tell the taxi driver where to go. They did not have a room yet, but knew in which section of the city they wanted to stay.

While Cynthia and the cab driver carried on a conversation in Spanish, Patti noticed that Cynthia kept glancing down at a piece of paper in her hand. Del was sitting on the edge of the seat. There was no other place to sit with all the baggage squashed in beside him. He motioned for Patti to look at the piece of paper in Cynthia's hand.

"Seventh-day Adventist Church" was written across the heading of the letter. Cynthia wanted to get a room in a hotel close to the church so they could go there the next day.

Seventh-day Adventist Church! That was their church! That is where she and Del wanted to go to church, too. Thank You, God. You truly are taking care of us on this trip.

The big church where Patti and Del accompanied Cynthia and Doug the next day had an English speaking class with a thought-provoking discussion. They enjoyed listening to people from a different culture. Patti would have liked for the class to last for hours. The sermon that followed was translated into English, and the congregation helped them feel that they were a part of the family.

Cynthia and Doug took Del and Patti to see many historical places they would never have tried to visit by themselves.

Cynthia translated for them at restaurants, museums, and other places of interest during that short, unforgettable mini vacation.

"O PRAISE the Lord, all ye nations: praise Him, all ye people. For His merciful kindness is great toward us; and the truth of the Lord endureth for ever. Praise ye the Lord." Psalms 117.

What would we have done without Cynthia and Doug? Patti and Del marveled as they visited famous sites, many museums, and beautiful places waiting to be explored. Only God could have arranged something so unexpected and fun.

What an awesome God!

34

Pioneering Again

Del had a dream that he had carried with him since a boy of twelve, when he lived by the rushing waters of Sykes Creek up in the mountains above Rogue River, Oregon. Someday he would own land in beautiful southern Oregon. On that land would be a dashing, tumbling creek—whose power he would harness. He would control that power to make electricity.

Although Del did live in the land of his youth, southern Oregon, still, he did not feel satisfied. He wanted to fulfill his boyhood dream. He found a "For Sale" sign on 40 acres of wilderness property, with a marvelous creek running through it. He determined to make that land his own.

Patti's father, 11 years past retirement age, realized the farm work had become too much for him and her mother. They were hoping to retire close to Patti and her family. At Del's suggestion, she agreed to move from the home she loved, to the wilderness property eight more miles from town. Her parent's farm was sold, her parents moved to Del and Patti's home, and she and Del moved to the wilderness. He already had a building constructed that they would live in until their new home was completed. Then he would use the building for a research lab.

On the forty acres of land, Del became a little boy again, pushing out roads and digging ditches. But now he looked much bigger, and his toys much, much, bigger. His D8 caterpillar and International backhoe tractor kept him busy and happy in the evenings, when he could arrange it.

With no telephone in the wilderness residence, he set up a CB. He also fixed one in Patti's parent's home. The CB squawked and said many things, but her parents never complained. Was Patti the only one complaining?

Pacific Power did not come near the property, so Del bought a generator. With one gallon of gasoline poured into the generator, it would make electricity for three hours—if it started. The wire that he ran to the car battery in the evening, worked to turn on one light bulb at night—if Del and the car happened to be home. The long plastic pipe he had laid up the mountain brought spring water into the little home—part of the time.

"What do you do for exercise?" Jean, Patti's cousin, asked on her way home from Hawaii.

Exercise? How could anyone wonder? It seemed that the only thing she accomplished was getting plenty of exercise. When she turned on the faucet and nothing happened, she got to go on a long walk up the mountain to the little spring to see why no water came to the house.

When the generator ran out of gas, she could always get exercise going through the darkness to fill it again, so she could work a little longer into the night.

When Del was home he did these things with gusto, but when was he home? He had read somewhere that exercise helped prevent discouragement, and since he seemed concerned about Patti, they went for morning walks wrapped in their raincoats and carrying flashlights. There were some things she definitely missed, but she did feel that it was **not** exercise.

Del had made a road just above the creek along the side

of the mountain. Patti enjoyed this beautiful place where one could watch the water tumbling over the rocks below.

This particular evening she took Sheba, her beautiful big German Shepherd with her, as she walked along above the creek. *God gives extravagantly*, she thought, as she looked at the wildflowers covering the hillside. *He spreads hundreds of little flowers over the terrain—although they are seldom even noticed.*

She listened to the birds getting ready for the night. *He gives the birds their winsome songs, and they sing their little hearts out—whether anyone listens or not.* She continued strolling up the road thinking, *I must not get discouraged. The best Gift from heaven would have come to die on the cross if only one person would have cherished that Gift. What love! What unlimited extravagance.*

The shadows had lengthened. Dusk began to cover the view. Patti switched on her flashlight. She watched Sheba take off after something and ran to see what it could be. When Sheba looked up in the tree, Patti looked also. A long tail swung back and forth above her head. Two big eyes peered down! Adrenalin and terror shot through Patti as she realized she was looking straight into the face of a crouching cougar! Slowly she began to walk backwards keeping her light on the animal. As soon as she felt she had gone far enough away, she called Sheba. They both ran for the house.

Patti saw a little black bear run across the road in front of her when she was driving home one evening. Del had seen it before when walking through the woods.

The most frightful thing was a rattlesnake. Patti stood still wondering what made the strange sound. Sheba came running to meet her and slid to a stop. The dog started jumping up and down barking furiously at something in the grass. Sheba kept the big rattler entertained until Ed got there.

Patti was not into killing snakes.

When they started to build their home, Del told her, "You may choose any house plan you like for our new home." She chose a chalet-type home. Del was appalled to see how the roof went this way and that way, but a promise is a promise. She made some changes. She added an upstairs balcony over the family room where a person could sleep at night, watch the stars, and listen to the singing creek.

Why have empty space over the garage? The area turned into a little library off one of the upstairs bedrooms. The half bath by the entry way was replaced by a full bath next to the garage.

Frank, Jean's husband, helped draw plans for an open, curved stairway—instead of the closed in one shown on the original plans.

Because the roof slanted so many directions, there were wonderful little attic rooms all over the place—extra storage off the bedrooms, off the balcony, and a big storage area above the downstairs bedroom. Patti's many ideas must have been a pain to Clarence, the excellent carpenter who worked to finish the house. However, she had never seen a more competent person in her life. His efficiency was only surpassed by his patience.

35

Was She An Angel?

The business never let up with the pressures it inflicted, but kept pushing Del and Patti to be three or four different places at once, while insisting they be home to look after things. By the 1980's, Del's electronic moisture detection instruments were no longer confined to the Northern Hemisphere. Patti lost her glasses in New Zealand. She left her billfold on the counter at the airport in Finland. The plane waited until the owner of the billfold was found and then soared into the icy sky.

Del and Patti traveled extensively—Canada, Mexico, Australia, and Europe.

"Watch the signs for a place to stay." Del and Patti were on a bus traveling through the hills in Germany, heading for a lumber mill, whose owner had purchased some of their equipment and requested that Del come look at some of his other plants.

"What are the signs supposed to say?" They had had a hard time finding which bus to take to get here. They did not know a word in German, and it seemed no one knew English out in this remote place—certainly not their bus driver.

"I really don't know. Maybe you can tell by the signs if there is a room or something at some place where we can stay for the night."

While winding around the hills, Patti watched the light disappear and darkness settle over the entire countryside. "Didn't Mr. Barknauff tell you where we should stay?"

Del was looking out the window. "No, but this is the town, and it looks as if we are already heading out of it."

Patti sent a quick SOS to heaven. *I know we were foolish not to have had better plans than this, but now what?*

"What will we do? Where will we stay tonight?" She must have been speaking more loudly than she thought for the bus became very quiet—painfully quiet. A lady standing at the front just ready to get off asked in perfect English, "Do you want a place to stay here tonight?"

"Yes," answered Del from the back of the bus where they were sitting.

"You should have gotten off at the last place then." She waited as the bus came to a stop.

"What should we do now?"

"Get off here with me, and I will tell you where to go."

Del and Patti began gathering their things as hastily as possible and followed the lady out into the night. As the bus pulled out, the lady pointed the way—she said they should go down this street until they got to that other street—*what name did she mention?*—then you turn—*which way was it?*—until you got to—*what did she say?*

"Oh, Del, do you know where to go?" Patti continued fighting back the tears. The night looked black.

"No. I thought you did."

"Catch her, Del. Catch her."

He took off on a run, and Patti stayed with their belongings. When Del and the lady came back, they were talking as if they were old friends. "You mean you don't speak any German?" she asked in dismay. "Oh, that is too bad. Then I must go with you and help you." Patti felt so relieved she thanked the lady over and over.

"When I was young, I lived in Canada for a few years," the lady told them. "It is hard being in a foreign country. There were some people who were very kind to me. Maybe this is one way I can help repay that deed."

When Del and Patti, with their new friend, finally arrived at the home having rooms for rent, the lady translated their message. Del paid the money for a night's lodging, and they were taken up the narrow stairway and shown the little room.

The next morning their smiling host guided them to a table. Coffee? Tea? Bacon? How does one say "no" in German? Patti thought they had declined, but soon the gracious hostess came in with both coffee and tea and a large plate of bacon. They did not have much else, but the bread tasted delicious, and not a crumb of it lay on the plate when they finished eating breakfast.

Patti went back upstairs while Del walked to the lumber mill. She read and rested in the chilly little room. It had pretty, yellow flowered wallpaper on the walls and looked spotlessly clean. She still felt overwhelmed with gratitude for the way the lady "just happened" to be getting off the bus where they needed to be.

The morning slowly became history, and half of the afternoon had passed, when Patti heard Del dashing up the stairs. He opened the door and exclaimed, "Hurry, Honey. Grab our things."

She always had the suitcases packed and ready to go—right by the door. He might be gone for hours, but with his appointment over, he would be moving fast, and today was no exception. The one and only afternoon bus going back to the city would be leaving any time. Patti had no desire to miss it.

The hanging bag and one suitcase that had shoulder straps were flung over Del's shoulders. He grabbed a suitcase in each hand, while she clutched her heavy purse and the treasures she had already purchased to take home.

Down the stairs, out the door, and across the road they rushed. Patti could not keep up, but she did not care. She knew if Del caught the bus, it would wait for her.

36

The Glass Door

As the bus sped down the road, Patti tried to see everything at the same time. She watched the chalet-type houses with bright flowers filling the planters beneath the windows flash by. The grounds around them looked as if they had been raked and tidied up before they ever needed it. Even the forests did not have brush or any dead, rotting logs among the trees.

When the bus came into the bus terminal, Del got a taxi to take them to the lovely place that had already been chosen for them. The reservations had been placed by someone at the mill where Del had an appointment the next morning.

The building looked like an old mansion. The long upstairs hall had a succession of rooms like sections of a telescope. Their sleeping room, at the end of the lengthy hall, had a wonderful bed, a dresser, and even a tiny bathroom snuggled off to one side.

A huge table, set for the evening meal, stretched the full length of the open dining room. Crusty loaves of bread, big bowls of fruit, and whatever else that had been put on the table took Patti's attention. Breakfast was only a distant memory.

After eating, Del decided to call Ed, now general manager of the business, to see how things were going. Forget about privacy. The only telephone in the building clung to the wall not far from the dining room table. A box-shaped something beside it told how long the call took and how much it was costing. With plenty of people around to help, Del finally got the complicated telephone system working. Ed was on the line.

"That company in Virginia is still having trouble," Ed told Del. "I think it is something you need to take care of."

Del talked with the repairman, while Ed called the company in Virginia, and got a telephone conference going.

Patti stared at the little box counting away their money. As Del continued to ask questions and give advice, people began getting up and coming over to look at the little box. They stood gazing at the figures as they went up, up, up! Soon almost everyone was whispering and talking—in German of course. Some seemed to get really excited while looking at the little box. Others looked disgusted. One man said something and threw his hands up in the air. He walked to the couch and put his head in his hands. Then he sat there shaking his head back and forth in utter dismay!

"How much is it costing?" Patti asked the man who seemed to be in charge of everything.

"It is already over two hundred twenty dollars in US funds," he gasped.

Would Del never quit? Finally he hung up the telephone and looked jubilant. "I think we worked out the problems with the WHK Sawmill in Virginia," he beamed. "You know, if I hadn't taken care of that bit of business, we would have had to cancel the rest of the trip and fly directly to Virginia."

"Do you know how much that phone call cost?"

"A lot less than a trip home."

"Del, we don't have enough money to pay for that phone call. I hadn't planned to spend that much for the rest of our stay in Germany."

Del went to talk to the man who looked as if he had just let something terrible happen. It appeared that Del said the right thing, for soon the stricken look was wiped from the man's face, and he began smiling.

"I'll have a taxi waiting first thing in the morning," Patti heard the man tell Del.

What does Del plan to do?

"Someone will call a taxi for you in the morning. You can go to the bank and cash your cashier's checks," Del explained. "If you can get that taken care of, we can be on our way when I get back from my appointment."

"Me?"

"Why not?"

Patti felt very alone and conspicuous the next morning, after breakfast, while walking through the fairly crowded room. People still sat at the table. Others were sitting on the couch or the chairs that were scattered around the area. She felt as if the eyes of the whole crowd were upon her and all were thinking, *Crazy Americans, who come to Germany and then spend so much money just to talk to the people they left behind.*

Patti, looking back, tried to be friendly and smiled at all those people watching her, while she continued to walk to the open (she thought) door and the taxi waiting outside. *Why did everyone have a questioning, startled expression?*

Bang!!

A massive plate glass door hit her across her whole body. Her head throbbed. She saw three people jump at the same time to come to her assistance. She had no idea what they were saying. The tone of their voices, and the look on their faces, told her they were much concerned about her well being. One man held the heavy, *invisible* glass door open, while someone else helped her put herself back together.

Why do these German people keep their windows and doors so clean, a person doesn't even know they are there? Yes, she did hurt a little physically, but her dignity had been shattered. Patti hurried to the taxi hoping the driver had not seen her smash herself right into the plate glass door.

The taxi driver spoke English. They talked about anything and everything they could think of to talk about on the way to the bank. He stopped in front of a large, modern building.

"I will be waiting right here for you," he told Patti.

She hastily entered the bank and stood awaiting her turn. Then she gave the cashier checks and passport to the bank teller. He picked them up and walked to the back of the room to talk to someone. They talked for awhile; two more people came over to join them. Patti waited while the four people stood at the back of the room examining her papers.

The taxi driver came in, and seeing her still standing at the window told her he was waiting outside. "Don't worry." He tried to comfort Patti. "I don't mind waiting."

Of course he didn't mind waiting. The rest of the money she had would probably go to pay his fees.

Patti had been in the bank over half an hour before a lady came over. "Is this an 'I' or an 'E?' " she asked.

"An 'E,' " Patti replied.

The lady joined the group standing in the back of the room. They scattered to their various jobs, and Patti was handed all of her ID papers along with the money she had requested.

An "I" or an "E"? That is what had taken a half hour?

Patti handed the taxi driver the small fee he asked, and hurried to the privacy of her room away from questioning eyes and people with whom she could not communicate. She laid her throbbing head on the fluffy pillow, and with the snowy white comforter around her, drifted off to sleep.

The next thing she knew, her husband came dashing into the room. "Gus, the man I have been working with at the mill, has taken the afternoon off to show us the country. He is waiting outside right now in his car. Would you like to see the Berlin Wall?"

37

A Foolish Mistake

Patti sprang from the bed with the triviality of her former problems vanishing like the morning fog.

"We are going sightseeing for the whole afternoon?" She hurried to get ready.

"Yes." Del started laughing at her exuberance.

She rode in the back of the car enjoying the adventure while watching the landscape flow behind them. Del and Gus sat in the front talking about lumber mills and other boring topics.

At the crest of one of the small rounded mountains, Gus stopped the car and motioned across the valley. Spread out before them were rolling green fields, attractive white houses, and a great wall separating the country. From where they were sitting, they could see on both sides of the wall. Gus explained how the farm had been divided. He pointed out where on one side of the wall was a brother with his immediate family, and on the other side lived his parents and the rest of the family. Patti could not help but comment on the dreadful isolation the people must be experiencing.

"Okay, let me show you something else." Gus spoke in subdued tones as he started the car and headed down the road again.

They drove for miles with Gus pointing out sights of interest to Del and Patti. Then he drove down a road with a large parking lot at the end. "This is where the wall goes right through a house."

Gus parked the car, and the three of them walked down to a huge wall. Del and Patti could not see over the other side of the wall from this location, but looked in awe and amazement at an impressive, but apparently vacant house that had been cut in half with the enormous wall going through the middle of it.

Patti stood almost spellbound by the things she had seen that day. She remembered when she was a little girl in the fifth grade promising that someday, she would travel. Someday she would visit every state in the United States. Through the years she had colored the correct space on a special map for each state she had had the privilege of being in. She had been able to visit every state in the United States, and now that dream was history.

But this—getting to see the things she had been seeing on the trip and especially today seeing the Berlin Wall—was exceeding all expectations. *Wait until she told the folks back home that she had touched the Berlin Wall!*

Patti stepped away from the people gazing in silent wonder at the wall before them. She walked over the rough terrain to the massive structure, put out her hand, and touched it. Then she turned and started back to Del and Gus.

Gus stepped forward, and the look on his face was—well—it was—Patti could not tell. *Embarrassed? Frightened? Angry? Confused? Maybe all those mixed up in one.*

"You just got your picture taken." Gus' tone sounded like he was scolding her.

"What do you mean?" Patti questioned innocently.

"Just look," he retorted.

She looked. She had been so engrossed in the majestic house that rested in secret silence with a massive wall through its middle, that she had not noticed the round guard tower on top of the wall. Looking up, she saw the guard. She saw the gun. She also saw that she was the center of the angry man's attention.

"Let's get out of here." Gus spoke to Del and Patti very quietly. They slowly hurried to the car with a calmness born of panic. Gus had the automobile miles down the road before anyone spoke!

Patti tried to calm the butterflies in her stomach and swallow her heart that seemed to be stuck in her throat. *This was more dangerous than smashing into a plate glass door!* To break the silence, Gus said, "Did you know we really have more freedoms over here in Germany than you do in America?"

"Do you really think so?" questioned Del.

"Sure we do." Gus grinned. "You have speed limits and can drive only certain speeds in America. We can drive as fast as we want to here on the Autobahn." He stepped on the gas. Patti could not tell how fast they were going from where she was sitting, but she didn't care. They were putting distance between themselves and that disheveled guard who gave her the impression that he was ready to kill her.

Maybe that fellow did have her picture, but if he wanted to see this lady again, he would have to come clear to America to do it.

When the big plane rolled to a stop in Atlanta, Georgia, Patti felt that she was nearly home. It felt good to touch American soil again. Never before had she appreciated her wonderful freedom in the good old USA and her wilderness home like she appreciated it now.

38

Home

Water hurrying down the slope through a ten inch pipe buried along the mountainside brought electricity into Del and Patti's new home. People came from miles to see the hydroelectric plant, and Del would explain it in detail above the roar of the Pelton Wheels located inside the powerhouse building. He showed where the water shot out of the pipe and cascaded down a cement chute, before it went tumbling through the waterway back into the creek. With everything working, there was plenty of electricity to heat the house and Del's large shop during the winter months when the creek was full of water.

Patti knew that they needed more electricity during the dry summer months than the creek could produce when it turned from a rushing torrent into a lazy little stream winding its way around the shallow rocks on its journey to the ocean. There would not be enough power for her to bake, wash clothes, or even run enough burners at the same time to get a good meal. Del talked with Pacific Power and found that it would cost six thousand dollars to run an electric line to their property.

"We really don't need it." He tried to convince Patti how wonderful home-made electricity really was. To make her happy, he did pick up the contract to have Pacific Power dig a ditch and lay the power line to the place. There was a deadline when the contract had to be signed, and the days and weeks and even a month slipped by.

"When are we getting the contract with Pacific Power signed?" She had asked this question a dozen times, but there were always more pressing things that had to be done.

"Where is that contract? We must do something about it!!" Patti felt an urgent need to get it signed and back to Pacific Power.

Del pulled the contract from the desk drawer. "Oh, no. It looks like today is the last day to get it in!"

Patti's heart almost stopped. "Let's go right now."

"I can't. I have an appointment with Mr. Anderson in fifteen minutes. He is coming clear from Idaho."

"Then sign, and give me the contract." Patti rushed to the car with the contract in her hand. She hated this car. They had taken it to the mechanic many times, but no one could figure out why it stopped for no reason and refused to run. Sometimes it just had no power, and a person had to creep along, and then stop and wait awhile, before going on again. The salesmen had stopped using it, and this car was the only one available for her. She made it to the freeway and then going up a small hill the car started losing power. It went so slowly she drove on the shoulder of I-5 while the other cars whizzed by.

"Oh, God, please just make this car keep going." It did keep going, mile after mile about fifteen miles an hour or less. By now Patti's watch said it was nearly four o'clock and Pacific Power closed at five. How could this be happening? "Please, God, just help me get there in time." Patti prayed the prayer over and over. When the car finally got to the middle of Grants Pass, it stopped. No amount of coaxing would get it going again. Her heart was racing. She could hardly think! Time was being lost!! "I can't waste any more of my time!" She had to get to Pacific Power by five o'clock!

The car was already sitting on the edge of the road, so Patti jumped out with the contract in her hand and started running for the Pacific Power office clear on the outer edge of town. Block after block she ran. Was she really doing this—but—who cared what people thought? Across the bridge, up a hill, across the main road, on and on she ran. It was already five o'clock. Would the door be locked? Three minutes after five Patti slid into the office, red faced, with perspiration running down her forehead. The manager stared at her with concern written all over his countenance.

"I hope I got here in time!?" She could hardly talk, but handed him the contract and slumped to a chair. After catching her breath, Patti asked to use the telephone and called Del to please come get her. She blurted out the whole exhausting story to Del over the telephone, while the man at Pacific Power waited. When she hung up the receiver, the man smiled at her and said, "Yes, you got here in time."

Six years before, after finishing engineering at Walla Walla College, Ed had turned down a good job offer. He had told his dad he would help in the business for two years before going into his own profession. Those two years kept expanding and so did the business. Under Ed's management, the equipment, the office, everything became computerized. A new generation was in charge.

Judy had gone to Walla Walla College to get her B. S. in nursing—and also met and fell in love with the man of her dreams, Michael Blair. Mike was a special person. They were proud to have him as a son-in-law. After the beautiful wedding, Mike and Judy lived in Corvallis where Mike earned his Masters Degree in business.

One day when Patti and the pastor's wife were visiting, she said to Patti, "I know a nurse in Portland whom I want Ed to meet. Maybe they won't even like each other. One thing I do know—both Ed and my friend, Linda Andregg, are brilliant people, so they will at least have something to talk about." Ed's car wore out its' tires going to Portland and back after that introduction.

As Patti sat in the church during Ed and Linda's lovely wedding, she thanked God for answering her many prayers. Ed was getting a wonderful wife. They were getting a wonderful daughter-in-law.

Del enjoyed being back into what he loved—research. The shop, where they lived while building their house had become a research lab with high-tech equipment. Del plunged into figuring out how to do things that most people thought could never be done, while in the winter his own hydroelectric plant busily made electricity for everything he needed.

Patti felt happy working at home again. Many times, looking up at the sky and seeing a jet going over, she thanked her Heavenly Father that her feet were on solid ground. Now she had a little time to do as she pleased. She pulled out her writing pad buried beneath the ups and downs of the years of experiences. Her pen could still write stories, articles, and poems, but this time she went to her computer and wrote—

The future is before us
Without a smudge or spot,
And we can trust it to our God
Without a worried thought.
Each day God gives a new page
As clean and white as snow.
What will fill the pages?
Only God can know.
Oh, God, with You beside us
In everything we do,
We'll face each new tomorrow
Holding onto You.

INVISIBLE LEADERSHIP STORIES

By Evelyn Wagner

STORIES MY DADDY TOLD ME begins the series with Evelyn's great-great-grandfather, a Scottish soldier, being shipped to America from Scotland to join the British in the American Revolution. Instead, he and his companions joined George Washington and fought to help free the new country from the British rule. Evelyn's great-grandfather sailed around the world many times placing American Ambassadors in other countries. Follow God's leading in the life of her grandfather as he joined a wagon train to go west, became a friend of the great leader Chief Sitting Bull, and later learned to know the God Who had been leading all his life. Watch as God saved her father and family from thieves, financial failure, and potential robbers.

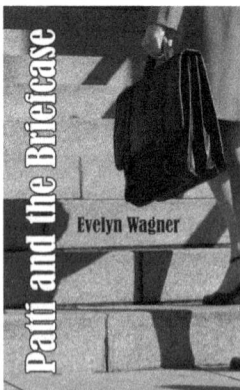

PATTI AND THE BRIEFCASE tells stories of a very shy bride going to Canada with her new husband to sell books. Stories too frightening and embarrassing for Evelyn to tell using her real name, she uses the name "Patti," the pet name her father called her when she was just a little girl.

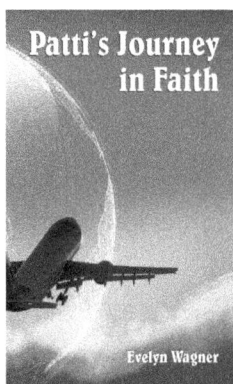

PATTI'S JOURNEY IN FAITH begins at Walla Walla College (University now) with a young couple named Delmer and Evelyn, but known as Del and Patti, in this setting. Travel with them in their struggle to serve their Lord in the challenges of going to college and then starting a new business. This story reveals a life of love, courage, disappointment, laughter, and discovery with the overarching theme of the gracious nearness of God.

FORWARD was the only way to go when Delmer and Evelyn stepped out in faith to start Christian television stations. God opened doors while the enemy built walls that seemed to shut down all progress. Watch God perform miracles when His people are willing to step FORWARD in faith.

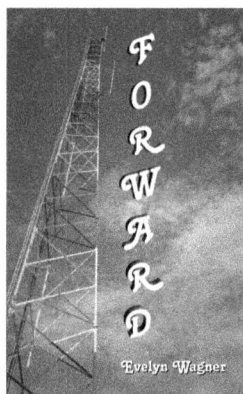

We invite you to view the complete
selection of titles we publish at:

www.TEACHServices.com

Scan with your mobile
device to go directly
to our website.

Please write or email us your praises, reactions, or
thoughts about this or any other book we publish at:

TEACH Services, Inc.

P U B L I S H I N G

www.TEACHServices.com

P.O. Box 954
Ringgold, GA 30736

info@TEACHServices.com

TEACH Services, Inc., titles may be purchased in bulk
for educational, business, fund-raising,
or sales promotional use.
For information, please e-mail:

BulkSales@TEACHServices.com

Finally, if you are interested in seeing
your own book in print, please contact us at

publishing@TEACHServices.com

We would be happy to review your manuscript for free.